THE
KABBALAH
OF
WRITING

"Sherri Mandell is brilliant, captivating, and relentlessly honest. Her book is a must for anyone who loves to write and wants to learn to write better."

BRIAN KILEY, COMEDIAN, EMMY AWARD–WINNING WRITER, AND HEAD MONOLOGUE WRITER FOR CONAN O'BRIEN

"Sherri Mandell takes us on a breathtaking journey through the spiritual energy of the ten sefirot and shows how each one opens a new doorway into the practice of writing. This is a world where kindness honors our inner voices, boundaries help us edit and focus, and harmony creates moments of insight. Mandell collects guidance from poets, essayists, psychologists, philosophers, and sages alike in a conversation that engages literary wisdom with sacred texts. Bursting with wisdom and practical advice, inspiration and writing prompts, Mandell shows us how to reveal and give voice to our own unique stories."

JANE MEDVED, AUTHOR OF *DEEP CALLS TO DEEP* AND *OLAM, SHANA, NEFESH* AND POETRY EDITOR OF THE *ILANOT REVIEW*

"*The Kabbalah of Writing* is rich with the most practical suggestions for writers, simple to follow, and abundant with possibility. Mandell shows us by example how to live a reading and writing life every day. Her book is a welcome guide for anyone seeking to link spiritual growth with literary experiment."

ILANA M. BLUMBERG, PH.D., AUTHOR AND ASSOCIATE PROFESSOR OF ENGLISH AT BAR-ILAN UNIVERSITY

"The Tree of Life is a map of the Divine's creative process, and a core Kabbalistic teaching is that we are partners with the Divine in completing and perfecting our part in that process. Sherri Mandell has given writers a great gift as she teaches us how to use the Tree of Life in our creative process, revealing our work to be the holy partnership that it is and enabling us to reach new creative depths and heights."

MARK HORN, AUTHOR OF *TAROT AND THE GATES OF LIGHT*

"I have never read a book that accomplishes so many goals without overwhelming the reader or oversimplifying the material. *The Kabbalah of Writing* incorporates a serious treatment of the sefirot interspersed with an illuminating survey of 'writers writing about writing,' peppered with personal anecdotes that warm the heart, and topped with an adventurous array of writing exercises."

SARAH YEHUDIT SCHNEIDER, AUTHOR OF *KABBALISTIC WRITINGS ON THE NATURE OF MASCULINE AND FEMININE*

"Highly original, beautifully conceived, *The Kabbalah of Writing* is a gift not only to aspiring writers but to anyone seeking to enhance their creative and spiritual potential."

YOSSI KLEIN HALEVI, SENIOR FELLOW AT THE SHALOM HARTMAN INSTITUTE

"Such poetic, light, penetrating wisdom riffles through these pages like an evening breeze in Jerusalem. This book contains just about everything I need to know to write better and live more richly."

RUCHAMA KING FEUERMAN, AUTHOR OF *IN THE COURTYARD OF THE KABBALIST*

"This book is a psycho-spiritual manual that applies the wisdom of the sefirot to the sacred art of creative writing. Freewheeling anecdotes, from personal experience, from Torah, and a multitude of celebrated writers, are sure to help us live more deeply, with greater courage and humor."

JEAN-PIERRE WEILL, AUTHOR OF *THE WELL OF BEING*

THE
KABBALAH
OF
WRITING

Mystical Practices for Inspiration and Creativity

SHERRI MANDELL

Inner Traditions
Rochester, Vermont

Inner Traditions
One Park Street
Rochester, Vermont 05767
www.InnerTraditions.com

SUSTAINABLE FORESTRY INITIATIVE — Certified Sourcing
www.sfiprogram.org
SFI-00854

Text stock is SFI certified

Cataloging-in-Publication Data for this title is available from the Library of Congress

ISBN 978-1-64411-610-4 (print)
ISBN 978-1-64411-611-1 (ebook)

Printed and bound in the United States by Lake Book Manufacturing, Inc. The text stock is SFI certified. The Sustainable Forestry Initiative® program promotes sustainable forest management.

10 9 8 7 6 5 4 3 2 1

Text design by Priscilla Harris Baker and layout by Debbie Glogover
This book was typeset in Garamond Premier Pro with Gill Sans, Tide Sans, and Optima used as display typefaces

Yehuda Amichai, excerpt from "Tourists" from *The Selected Poetry of Yehuda Amichai,* University of California Press, 2013. Reprinted by permission of University of California Press.

James Wright, excerpt from "A Blessing" from *Above the River: The Complete Poems and Selected Prose.* Copyright 1990 by James Wright. Reprinted by permission of Wesleyan University Press.

James Wright, excerpt from "Lying on a Hammock at William Duffy's Farm in Pine Island" from *Above the River: The Complete Poems and Selected Prose.* Copyright 1990 by James Wright. Reprinted by permission of Wesleyan University Press.

Larry Levis, excerpt from "Winter Stars" in *Winter Stars,* copyright 1985. Reprinted by permission of the University of Pittsburgh Press.

Terry Tempest Williams, excerpt from "A Letter to Deb Clow," from *Red: Passion and Patience in the Desert.* Originally appeared in *Northern Lights* magazine, summer 1998 edition. Reprinted by permission of Brandt and Hochman Literary Agents, Inc. All rights reserved.

Elizabeth Bishop, excerpt from "The Fish," from *Poems,* Farrar, Straus, and Giroux, 2011. Reprinted by permission of Farrar, Straus, and Giroux.

The author made every attempt to credit appropriately and seek permission, where necessary, for quotes used in this book. Any oversights or omissions will be corrected in future editions.

To send correspondence to the author of this book, mail a first-class letter to the author c/o Inner Traditions • Bear & Company, One Park Street, Rochester, VT 05767, and we will forward the communication, or contact the author directly at **www.kobymandell.org/sherri-mandell**.

Acknowledgments

I thank my devoted and talented students—Faigie Heiman, Rachel (Joanne) Ginsberg, Ellen Berkman Amzallag, Sharon Litvin, Debby Neuman, Shira Shreier, Frieda Woznica, Ruth Warzecha, Michelle Gordon, and Rebecca Weinberger—for the privilege of teaching you the past many years. My husband, Seth, is brilliant, unique, a fantastic husband, and the love of my life. Thank you for being my best friend and best adviser. And to my beautiful, funny sisters, Nancy Lederman and Loren Fogelson—I'm so glad that you are in my life.

I am grateful to my determined and insightful agent, Anna Olswanger, who helped me shape this book.

I am blessed with wonderful nieces and nephews and sisters-in-law and brothers-in-law.

I thank Avi Liberman for bringing Comedy for Koby to Israel, supporting the Koby Mandell Foundation, and making us laugh. Thanks Jeremy and Dena Wimpheimer for your hard work in producing the shows.

Thanks to Menachem and Dena Mendlowitz for opening your home and hearts to us.

Finally, I want to thank our children, Daniel, Eliana and Avraham, Gavi and Pliah, and our grandchildren, Ori, Yehuda, Levi, and Tzori, who bring us such joy.

CONTENTS

INTRODUCTION

WHEN I WAS TWENTY-SEVEN, after teaching freshman composition at Virginia Commonwealth University in Richmond on a one-year contract, I traveled to Spain, Morocco, and Israel by myself. One July night in 1984, a new friend and I hiked to a hot spring in Sefat, Israel, and submerged there in the darkness. It turned out that we weren't in a hot spring but in the *mikveh** of Rabbi Issac Luria, known as the Ari (which means "the Lion"), the mystic associated with the Kabbalah who shared his wisdom in Sefat in the sixteenth century. The Ari had lost his father as a child, was raised in Egypt by an uncle, and soon found his calling as a solitary seeker. He studied mystical teachings from the Zohar† and meditated for seven years on the shores of the Nile. Later, he became a revered teacher of Kabbalah, probing the mysteries of creation: How could an all-encompassing God contract himself to leave space for the world to exist? What is the task of human beings in a world suffused with divinity? Though the Ari did not choose to write, Rabbi Chaim Vital recorded the notes of the Ari's teachings and remarked: "He was expert in the language of trees, the language of birds and the speech of angels. He could read faces. He could discern all that any individual had done, and could see what they would do in the future."

---

*A ritual bath.
†The Zohar is an allegorical and mystical commentary of the Pentateuch that serves as the principal text of the Kabbalah.

There is a tradition that anybody who enters the mikveh of this inspired, holy sage returns to Judaism and a belief in the divine. I didn't believe it that night. I had a master's degree in creative writing. I'd graduated from Cornell. I had no need for religion. On the other hand, I knew nothing about my religion. I had no religious training—no bat mitzvah, no temple, no Sunday school, no connection to Israel, the Hebrew language, or the Bible. I had no inkling of the depth and beauty of Jewish spirituality. And once I learned about Judaism, I felt an undeniable attraction to it. I ended up staying in Israel, marrying a religious man, keeping Shabbat and kosher, going to synagogue, and learning to pray in Hebrew. Now I have lived in Israel for twenty-five years. I speak Hebrew with my daughter-in-law and son-in-law. My kids and grandchildren are Israelis.

When I began to teach creative writing in Jerusalem, it was natural that I would think about writing in a different way, in a spiritual way. I had by then learned about Kabbalah and the ten *sefirot,* channels or spheres that comprise the elemental spiritual structure underlying, infusing, and animating the world—the divine design. I suspected that the sefirot would offer a fundamental and fascinating structure for exploring the art of writing essays and memoir.

Thus this book was born. Here I explain the characteristics of the sefirot and provide writing exercises, in the hope that together we can access our creativity and allow for divine inspiration. By studying the sefirot, profound and essential avenues of God's expression, we touch the processes that are at the heart of all creation.

The Spiritual Truth of Writing

Writing is a means of appreciating the world, allowing us to pay attention and concentrate so that we notice and record the unique, sometimes fleeting truths that the divine sends to each of us, our stories.

Rabbi Pinchas, a pious man who lived in Lod, Palestine, in the second century, said, "A man's soul will teach him. There is no man who is not constantly being taught by his soul." One of Rabbi Pinchas's disciples asked: "If this is so, why don't men obey their souls?" Rabbi Pinchas explained, "The soul teaches constantly. But it never repeats" (Martin Buber, *Tales of the Hasidim: The Early Masters*).

Writing allows us to respect and remember those moments. That which is truly ours cannot be duplicated by another person, but it can be lost to us if we don't receive it and express and transform it by telling our stories. The word *sefira* (channel) is related to the Hebrew word *lesaper,* which means "to tell a story." Each of us has a unique, valuable story to contribute to the larger story of being. Writing becomes a pilgrimage to discover the sacred stories given to us: singular gifts of imagination that only we can reveal to the world through our writing, shining sparks of divinity, ideas and images and insights. Divine inspiration.

A Summary of the Sefirot

The first sefirot we will examine are *will, inspiration,* and *comprehension.* Almost every piece of writing is based on *will:* the writer's need to express or question or understand something pushes her to the written word. Next we allow for *inspiration,* both the small and large gifts we receive from the world as well as moments of frustration and anger that motivate us to express ourselves. We struggle for *comprehension:* What is it we are trying to say? What is being revealed to us through patterns and images that repeat, intersect, and transform themselves? We contemplate and imagine. We question, reflect, and engage with our text.

The next seven spheres, known as the more emotional ones, are *kindness, boundaries, harmony, endurance, surrender, creativity,* and *rulership.*

Kindness means that we honor our inner voices, give free rein to our expression, overflow with words, write without self-consciousness about what we love and hate, explore our passions and interests. But the need for *boundaries* enables us to contract—to pare down and edit in order to focus so that we can discover *harmony:* moments of insight.

Writing requires both *endurance*—perseverance and patience—as well as the ability and time to *surrender* to what the material wants to tell you because your writing will speak to you; your writing will tell you what you need to know. Close attention to your text will allow you to generate new material and insights. Even when you are not writing, your mind is in motion, sometimes in a dreamlike generative state. Your *creativity* becomes heightened.

You can think of *rulership* as a way of governing your material, realizing your own unique voice in this world, your own vision and authority. Rabbi Kook, the first rabbi of the state of Israel, says that "to believe in God is to believe that one's soul and character are God-given and must come to self-realization not only for one's own sake, but also for that of humanity and of God himself" (Yehudah Mirsky, *Rav Kook: Mystic in a Time of Revolution*). Telling one's story becomes an essential part of the spiritual evolution of the world.

Each *sefira* has its own character, but the sefirot also blend with one another, are tempered by one another, and arrive as mixtures. In fact, every sefira contains all of the others, and in most situations, we express a combination of the sefirot. For example, we accompany kindness with boundaries and limits because unbounded kindness can be destructive. Think of a parent who always gives to a child without saying no, and how that child will be damaged. For the sake of simplicity, I present each sefira as distinct but know that they are woven together in our world.

In this book we will examine the sefirot in terms of both form and content. For example, how does the form of the essay embody generosity, a characteristic of the sefira of kindness? What does generosity mean to you? What does it mean to you to set boundaries? What is the role of perseverance in your writing life? How have you learned to surrender?

This book focuses on memoir and essay writing because I am primarily a memoir writer. My first book, *The Blessing of a Broken Heart,* chronicled my struggles in dealing with the murder of my son Koby and won a National Jewish Book Award.

Writing is a process of thinking—it's how we know what we know—and this book is for anybody who wants to think about his or her writing, to improve it, to keep working on it, and to see it as a necessary spiritual mission. It's not surprising that the word *sefira* is also connected to *sapir,* the Hebrew word for "sapphire." Think of your stories as precious gems waiting to be mined, polished, and offered to the world. Use the techniques and exercises in this book to create a writing practice for yourself so that you can appreciate the richness of your life, retrieve its divine beauty, and share your unique wisdom.

WRITING EXERCISE: A WISH AND A PRAYER

Write a prayer or wish for yourself. You might want to keep this near your writing desk. What are your intentions, hopes, and dreams for yourself as a writer?

1

WILL

Keter

THE SEFIRA *KETER,* WHICH LITERALLY MEANS "CROWN," is the sphere that is closest to God and most distant from us. God's presence and power loom above us, but the meaning and mechanism of divine will are impossible for us to fathom. The world that God created is so majestic and complicated—simple and complex, imminent and transcendent—that it defies our comprehension. The big questions— what happens after death and before birth, the meaning of the soul, nature, and stars and galaxies, how the brain works, why there is a world at all—are simply beyond our grasp. As I write this the world is in the midst of the coronavirus crisis, which demonstrates our lack of control in this world. With all of our advances in science and technology, we are still at the mercy of forces we cannot always understand.

Will, however, reminds us that, no matter what, we are actors in the world who can choose the way we want to live. Even during the horrors of the Holocaust, there were those who refused to relinquish their personal power. Many helped friends or relatives in the concentration camps with them, sharing their meager rations, choosing to be as human as possible under horrifying conditions. Rabbi Menachem Schneerson, the most recent Lubavitcher rabbi who died in Brooklyn in 1994 and is still revered by his followers, said, "A person is where his will is." According to commentary in the Bible, wherever it says "and it came to pass" is a sign of impending tragedy because the characters are passive (Megillah 10B).* Activity, on the other hand, is the defeat of tragedy: wherever the Bible says "and there will be," is a sign of impending joy (Bamidbar Rabbah 13).†

If the narrator in our essays and memoirs ardently wants and desires, he is more inclined to be an actor in the story, to take an engaged role rather than be a passive victim who is buffeted and defeated by experience. In this way, the narrator becomes heroic, even if his heroism consists of the honesty with which he interprets the events in his life. When the narrator desires truth and refuses to be battered by events, the reader is more likely to stay interested in the narrator's struggles.

In this chapter we'll try to understand how will propels us to compose our lives in writing. We'll also look at an array of obstacles that prevent us from expressing our will in this world.

Desire

Desire is the hidden engine of will. We feel hungry and desire to eat, so we harness our will to make a meal. We desire to help a friend, so we engage our will and drive to his house and lend him our car. We love language and long to create, to express our being in the world. So we marshal our will and write.

It's important to understand your desire to write. What drives you to write? If you're writing to make money or for fame, you may have to wait a long time to achieve either of them. But if you're writing because you want to understand the world and yourself, if you need to compose your world through your writing—and I mean compose in both senses of the word, to arrange and re-create but also to calm and quiet—then writing itself becomes its own reward.

---

*Megillah is one of the five sacred books of the Ketuvim (writings), the third division of the Old Testament.
†Bamidbar Rabbah is a midrash of rabbinical interpretations of the Book of Numbers.

Of course, sometimes life presents such interesting stories that you want to grab them and hold on to them, examine them and share them. Yet many of us write because we have painful stories that need to be expressed, traumas that need to be addressed. We desire to share our stories, and we want to be listened to, not only to express our pain but also as a way to acquire wisdom and healing.

Sometimes we write because we are longing for something. The word *long* is derived from Old English *langian,* which means both to "grow long, prolong" and "dwell in thought, yearn." We long for something far away. We want. Yet, sometimes we don't even know what it is we are longing for. When the Hebrew people who left Egypt wandered in the desert and were given manna to eat, they did not have to labor for their food. The manna tasted like whatever the people imagined. Yet the people claimed that they craved the meat that they had eaten in Egypt. Some commentators say that they craved desire. They craved a craving. We are created to desire. When a person has no desire, it's often a sign of depression.

I understand that lack of desire. In 2001 my son Koby was murdered by terrorists when he was thirteen. He and his friend Yosef Ish Ran cut school and went hiking in the canyon near our home in Israel. They were accosted by terrorists who beat them to death with rocks. Of course, my life stopped even though I had three other kids and a husband and friends. I wanted to die. I had no desire because the only thing I wanted was to have Koby back. With a lot of support from my husband, friends, family, and my community and with the help of writing a spiritual memoir about our loss, I was able to return to life.

Longing is related to the word *belonging.* We search to feel connected, to feel part of something larger than us. We long to belong; we long for relationship, for love, for friends and family, for a community. Some of us yearn for a relationship with the divine, with the eternal. We want to feel God in our lives, to know what the divine wants from us, to see some sort of truth that is eternal and transcendent.

Desire is wired into us. It makes sense that narrative often grapples with longing and takes place in the gap between desire and fulfillment, in our stumbling attempts to achieve our desires. "Not to have is the beginning of desire," says the poet Wallace Stevens in *Notes toward a Supreme Fiction*. Our writing does not have to solve our desire; it only has to fully express it.

Sometimes a story is about a narrator who desires *not* to change, not to be affected by others. For example, in Raymond Carver's short story "Cathedral," the narrator eats and drinks himself numb, disdaining and mocking others—a classic wise-guy. But when a friend of his wife, a blind man, visits his home, the narrator is exposed to a world that is more meaningful, elevated, and loving. By the end of the story, the narrator finds himself late at night drawing a cathedral he sees on the television for the blind man, the blind man's fingers riding his own. The narrator recognizes something stirring beyond himself. In fact, the last statement of the narrator in the story is: "It's really something." The narrator has at last broken through the defenses that prevented him from feeling any lack in his life. He finally experiences something exalted and sacred beyond the barriers of his abrasive, defensive personality.

As readers, it's not just desire that interests us but the quality of that desire. If we write about searching for designer shoes, a reader may have a hard time relating to us. (Except if you're Nora Ephron. Let's face it: if a writer charms us or makes us laugh, we'll follow her anywhere.) Something important and emotionally urgent should be at stake. It helps to think of the issues you're writing about as life and death matters. That's why movies and TV shows are often battles of life against death, but emotional stakes can be just as urgent. In Alice Munro's stories, for example, characters often struggle with shame and betrayal.

My teacher, fiction writer Steve Almond, points out that in order for the reader to care about the main character in a story, the character also has to care passionately about something. In an essay the narrator becomes the character who wants and desires and cares. If the narrator doesn't care about something deeply, even desperately, then the reader won't care about the narrator.

WRITING EXERCISE: YOUR STORY

What is the story you wish you could read? What kinds of books do you like reading? Describe the memoir you would like to read in a few sentences. Perhaps that is the book that you could write.

In 1996 I had a burning desire—to save my father's life. Obviously, a lot was at stake.

That February, six months after my husband and I and our four children moved to Israel, my mother called me and told me that I should come home because my father wasn't doing well. He'd been diagnosed with thymoma, cancer of the thymus gland, a few months earlier. I flew from Israel where I left my husband and children and landed in West Palm Beach, Florida. I took a taxi to the white brick, two-bedroom apartment in the Pines of Delray Beach, Florida, because my mother could not leave my father to pick me up. He had endured an operation on his thymus gland. The tumor was removed, and he had been sent home. The doctor said he was fine; the operation was a success. The minute I saw him, a frail man who had only months before been strong and vital, I knew he was dying.

It was as if he were disappearing before our eyes. He couldn't eat. He weighed less than 120 pounds. The thought of food made him gag. My father had previously had a huge appetite. He would cook soups and stews for us, and he would have many servings. Now he sat in an upholstered lounge chair in the living room watching TV. He couldn't shift the back of the chair into a reclining position because he was so weak. One morning soon after, when a caretaker arrived, my mother and I drove to a furniture store to buy him a padded chair that would be more comfortable for his skeletal body.

We wanted him to eat, but he had no appetite. The HMO doctor finally prescribed Marinol, a marijuana pill to help his appetite. Frantic to help my father, my mother and I left my father at home and drove to every drugstore in Delray Beach and Boca Raton with the prescription, waited on long lines with gray-haired patrons in numerous pharmacies, but there were no Marinol pills available. Then I got the idea to call Roger, a boyfriend from high school who I knew was now living in Florida, to ask him if he knew where I could get marijuana. If I couldn't get the pills, I would try the real thing.

I don't recommend calling old boyfriends after twenty-five years. I stood in my mother's kitchen in front of the electric stove, the clock above me the square yellow one from my childhood. Roger's wife answered and gave me his number at the restaurant he managed. He was, of course, surprised to hear from me, especially since I hadn't spoken to him for a quarter of a century, and here I was asking him for marijuana. But he said that he would do what he could and get back to me. I didn't hear from him. But late that night, I answered the phone at my mother's house, and an angry voice asked for me: "Who the hell do you think you are? What are you doing calling my husband? Don't you dare call my husband for narcotics. I'll send the cops to your house."

She hung up on me. I told my mother that Roger's wife had threatened me. We laughed nervously and locked the front door.

The gap between my frantic desire to save my father's life and the wife who thought I was out to corrupt or steal her husband is the backbone of an essay.

By the way, we finally obtained the Marinol, and my father ate a bowl of chocolate ice cream. We watched TV that night in my parents' bedroom, my father in his new chair, me lying on the bed. While we were watching the evening news, my father laughed and said: "I can't tell if I'm watching a comedy or a tragedy." I felt like he had reached an elevated spiritual truth, similar to the state that people are supposed to feel on Purim, the holiday that celebrates the salvation of the Jews in the days of the Persian empire. What was supposed to be the extermination of the Jews proved to be their deliverance. On the holiday there is a commandment to eat and drink until you don't know the difference between evil and good.

───

Writing Exercise: Desire

Writer and critic Charles Baxter describes a literary scene as *the staging of a desire.*

- Write about something you desired as a child or young adult. What happened?
- What is your greatest desire today? What steps could you take toward fulfilling that desire? What prevents you from working toward fulfilling that desire? What would happen if you achieved it? Write in the present tense.

───

Encouragement

The sefira keter is related to faith. We want to have faith that our stories matter, yet it is very easy to be discouraged. I've had many students tell me about English teachers who criticized them. Sometimes it is only after twenty-five years that they find the courage to write again.

Once, a few years ago, I was tap dancing in Philadelphia in a park—just for fun—while I was on a book tour. An older woman walked by me and said: "Aren't you too old to do that?" Talk about a slap in the face. And I didn't even know her. Why is it that we remember when someone has judged us harshly? So many of us can tell stories of people who damaged our desire and talents in some way.

Yet it is important to recognize the people who support us. Archie Ammons, a Pulitzer Prize–winning poet, my creative writing professor at Cornell University, encouraged me to keep writing. I wasn't an English major like most of the other students in my class. Instead, I was in the agriculture school studying natural resources, ecology. One day toward the end of the semester, Professor Ammons asked me to read all of the poems I had written that semester aloud to the class, all ten poems. After I read each poem, he said: *read another poem.* And then, *another.* He nodded after each poem. "I like that," he said.

He helped me keep my will to write alive. I notice with many of my students that there is often a teacher in their past who has been a mentor and told them that they have talent. Sometimes all we need is a little encouragement. Who in your life has encouraged you?

WRITING EXERCISE:
DISCOURAGEMENT AND ENCOURAGEMENT

- Write about somebody who discouraged you. What did this person say to you? How did they harm you? Tell us. Now write back to them. Let it all out. Tell them what you couldn't say then.

- Now write about somebody who encouraged you. What did this person's encouragement mean to you? Encouragement includes the word courage, which is derived from the word for "heart." In what way did they give you heart?

- How do you encourage yourself? How do you listen to your own needs and desires and cheer yourself on? Do you have a voice inside of you that provides a sense of support?

- You might also want to write about the encouragement that you provide to other people. Who in your life do you encourage? Try to describe a specific incident.

The Writing Process

In order to write, we need to engage our will, but there's an important distinction between will and willpower. I always make myself a cup of tea as an incentive to trick myself to start working. Writing can be a difficult, occasionally excruciating experience, but it can also be calming and pleasurable. Annie Dillard, who won the Pulitzer Prize for her book *Pilgrim at Tinker Creek* and has written many other books, says that "writing a book is like rearing children—willpower has very little to do with it. If you have a little baby crying in the middle of the night, and if you depend only on willpower to get you out of bed to feed the baby, the baby will starve. You do it out of love. Willpower is a weak idea; love is strong. . . . Caring passionately about something isn't against nature, and it isn't against human nature. It's what we're here to do."

In other words, the will to write comes from love. We love language and seek patterns and coherence in our work. With time, often a lot of time, we learn to crave the solitude of writing, connecting to and nourishing an inner voice that emerges on the page. On the other hand, our need to write can also stem from anger or jealousy or from simple persistence. Writing is an opportunity to take the passion and love inside you and focus it, transform it, and share it with a reader. What do you care about passionately? What do you find intolerable? Tell the world.

WRITING EXERCISE:
PASSION AND WILLPOWER

- What role has willpower played in your life? When did you try to exercise willpower and how did the experience turn out?
- What is your passion today? What do you love or hate? Write about it.

Obstacles

Each sefira has a quality that opposes it. Doubt blocks will and desire. Doubt can prevent us from defining and expressing our will in the world. Almost all of us doubt ourselves at times, some people more than others. We doubt our worth, our right to speak. Who will care about our thoughts and ideas, our stories? We're afraid we're wrong or we'll make a mistake. We're afraid to stick up for ourselves. And if we do write, we may not believe in the validity or power of our expression. Whenever my students share their work aloud in class, for example, they almost always start with disclaimers like these:

> It's just totally nothing.
> I'll read it, but it's really not very good.
> I didn't have a lot of time.
> I didn't do it the way it's supposed to be done.
> I didn't know what I was supposed to write.
> I really don't think this is very interesting.
> I don't know why I wrote this.
> I don't like what I wrote at all.

I tell my students: no more disclaimers, no apologies. But they still want to apologize. I do, too, when I share my work. It's hard to take ownership of our intimate expression. We want our work to be interesting, intelligent, and playful, but we are so imperfect. We fear exposing parts of ourselves that we would prefer to keep hidden. We may feel like imposters. Yet writing demands a large degree of exposure.

It's important to know that doubt does not always have to be extinguished or vanquished. Expressing doubt can be a useful technique for writing essays because it's authentic, and when we disclose our worries, we're vulnerable and real. It's when doubt paralyzes us because we don't have the courage to talk back to it and overcome it, when it stops us rather than challenges us, that it becomes destructive.

In fact, vulnerability allows us to be soft and to wonder in both senses of the word. To look at the world with wonder. And to wonder as a reflective action. To wonder how things could have been different, for example. To wonder how we became the person we are.

⌒

WRITING EXERCISE:
DOUBTS AND VULNERABILITY

- Create a list of all of the reasons that you can't write. Let them all out, all those negative critical voices that live inside you.
- Now write a letter to that cramped, narrow part of yourself—the judgmental, critical, nasty voice that says that you have nothing to say and no right to say it. Tell that voice off, put it in its place. Stand up to that voice and say: *I am going to do this anyway. I will be faithful to my calling.*
- Write about a doubt that you had, an experience where you vacillated between two opinions. Let yourself be of two minds: on the one hand this, on the other that; maybe this, maybe that. Don't decide anything.
- Write an essay about a time when you felt vulnerable. Include sentences like this: "I don't like to admit that . . ." or "It's hard for me to admit that . . ."

⌒

The Fear of Narcissism

Another obstacle to implementing our will to write is our fear of egotism. Some writers fear their own self-importance: Why should my ego take center stage? Some are afraid to write because they think it means that they're selfish, taking the time to express their inner life. In this age of Twitter, Facebook, Instagram, and TikTok, when everyone has a blog and a person's every move, meal, and meeting is documented, this may seem an outdated concern. And yet, if you are serious about your vocation as a writer, you or others may question your intent. Who are you to carve out time for yourself to sit and write? Who are you to voice your opinions, ideas, imagination? Who are you to pay attention to your will to think and write?

In the introduction to *The Art of the Personal Essay: An Anthology from the Classical Era to the Present,* Philip Lopate points out that the well-known essayist and writer E. B. White, author of *Charlotte's Web* and *Stuart Little,* grappled with the issue of egotism. White wrote:

> I think some people find the essay the last resort of the egoist, a much too self-conscious and self-serving form for their taste; they feel that it is presumptuous of a writer to assume that his little excursions or his small observations will interest the reader. There is some justice in their complaint. I have always been aware that I am by nature self-absorbed and egotistical; to write of myself to the extent I have done indicates a too great attention to my own life, not enough to the life of others. I have worn many shirts, and not all of them have been a good fit. But when I am discouraged and downcast I need only fling open the door of my closet, and there, hidden behind everything else, hangs the mantle of Michel de Montaigne, smelling slightly of camphor.

Montaigne, who lived in France in the sixteenth century, is known as the first modern essayist because his essays trace the meandering stream of his own consciousness. Some may find him tiresome, yet Montaigne is always citing other writers, having a conversation with other voices, even when he is speaking about himself.

So even when self-absorbed, if a writer is in conversation with what others have said and has the ability to look beyond himself, if he is curious, then though he is writing about himself, he is also expanding the reach of his own consciousness and awareness. And ours. Opening a larger window to the world. I tell my students to look at the bigger picture: How does their personal experience fit into a larger context? Essays that are a conversation with what others have written or thought about the subject are often the most powerful and interesting. The writer is not alone. As T. S. Eliot writes in "Tradition and the Individual Talent": "No poet, no artist of any art, has his complete meaning alone. His significance, his appreciation is the appreciation of his relation to the dead poets and artists."

While you are writing, read other books that pertain to your topics and see how they inform your text. You can include biblical, mythological, or other literature that parallels, amplifies, or contrasts with the meaning of your own story. Connect to history or what is happening in the outside world as you write. Quote or paraphrase other writers and thinkers in your essays. Engage with what other people have said, but add your unique perspective. Readers want to know your story.

WRITING EXERCISE: RESPONDING TO LITERATURE

Kathleen Hill's memoir *She Read to Us in the Late Afternoons: A Life in Novels* interweaves her own life experience with literature that mirrors and focuses her life experiences. Pick a book that has profound meaning for you and respond to its themes or its language in an essay.

WRITING EXERCISE: AN OUTLINE FOR YOUR MEMOIR

Write your autobiography in one page, a list of ten experiences or turning points that comprise your personal history. This isn't a résumé but an emotional or spiritual history, events that shaped your being and caused you to change. Make a list of those events that call you to write about them because they have emotional heat rising from them. Writing teacher Lisa Dale Norton calls these "shimmering images." One way of shaping each experience into a series of essays is to focus on desire as well as conflict. What did you want? What did you get? What occurred as a result of or despite your will and desire? Return to these experiences when you need writing ideas. They can form the rough outline of a memoir.

INSPIRATION

Chochmah

WE OFTEN BEGIN WRITING BECAUSE SOMETHING INSPIRES US, touches us or interests us. We're curious, open to experience. The word *inspiration* derives from the Latin *inspirare*, "breathe or blow into." In the Torah we are told that man was created by God by breathing or blowing into him. "And God formed man, dust of the ground, and breathed the breath of life into his countenance and so man became a living being." Inspiration is sourced in the divine.

Inspiration gives us the gift of being alert to our world: divinity may be hiding anywhere. Too often we belittle the topics that surround us. For example, we may not think it worthwhile to write essays about the tedious aspects of raising children or doing laundry or driving to work. But almost anything—a game of touch football or weeding in the garden—can become an opening to a larger truth.

In her essay "The Death of the Moth," Virginia Woolf observes a moth fluttering about her windowpane, which leads her to reflect on the overwhelming majestic powers of life and death. She wonders about death choosing a common moth as an adversary.

When we pay attention to the glory and mystery of the ordinary, we enter our lives more fully. We may collect bits of experience and ideas that inspire us—from our reading, thinking, and activities—which can then be woven together in a way that surprises us. This amassing of material, almost like raking or gathering, can feel like a form of divine supervision or *hashgacha pratit,* which means "divine providence." The image or information you need for your essay appears as if by magic. An idea for your essay floats into your head when you're walking or listening to a podcast. Sometimes the best creative gifts are small ones that we receive when we are not expecting anything, like the Ferris wheel that I noticed last week when I drove near my home, which had magically appeared on the horizon, delighting me with its sudden unlikely appearance.

We may think that we have to write about dramatic events and wait for them to occur, when all around us, still, small stories wait to be noticed and recorded. In the Book of Kings, we learn about Elijah, a fiery prophet who fights against idol worship and who is also a miracle worker, able to travel between this world and the next. Yet when Elijah meets the divine, God is not in the mighty wind or the earthquake or the fire that God sends to him. God is in a still small voice.

In this chapter you'll learn about inspiration—how it can be sourced in the mundane or in beauty or in discomfort. Yet the nature of inspiration can be problematic: it is exciting and attractive, even compelling, yet uncontrollable and evanescent.

Writing Exercise: Small Gifts

Write about something small that happened to you this week that might have just passed you by, that you might have forgotten. It could be something simple, like the way the sun rose so early and its blazing light was so overwhelming that it woke you at three-thirty in the morning. You could write about a change in the landscape, a conversation that you had with your son, or a decision that you needed to make. You could write about the way people wait for a bus. Try to sense what was unique in the experience, its small and shining significance.

Curiosity

Inspiration is often sourced in curiosity. *Chochmah* literally means "the power of what." *Mah hu:* What is this? In an essay called "Wonderlust," Tony Hiss speaks about deep travel, the ability to journey somewhere new and see vividly and wonder: What is this thing that my mind or eyes or ears alight on? What does it look like? Smell like? Sound like? Feel like? What does it remind me of? What is it made of? How did it get here? Deep travel doesn't require a trip to India or New Zealand or Africa—which is lucky since as I'm writing this, very few planes are flying because of the coronavirus.

Writing can provide an opportunity to immerse ourselves in the present so that we see things as if we've never seen them before. Maybe this is close to what Keats refers to as negative capability: "when a man is capable of being in uncertainties, mysteries, doubts, without an irritable reaching after fact and reason." We see differently because we shed our preconceptions and certainties. We reject the commonplace. In her poem "The Summer Day," poet Mary Oliver wonders if this close attention is a form of prayer.

⟶

WRITING EXERCISE:
OBSERVING AND APPRECIATING

Inspiration can be found in nature and in the everyday: "Today is the day that God created. Let us rejoice and be glad in it" (Psalm 118).

- Take a walk in nature and observe your surroundings. Use your senses. What does a small slice of nature look like, smell like, feel like? Listen to it. Touch it. What do you see that you never saw before? Write a detailed description.
- Write about something that you are inspired by today in the present tense. You can describe an unexpected moment of beauty or insight.

⟶

Insecurity as Inspiration

As beauty can serve as inspiration, so can our insecurities. Robert Atwan, series editor of *The Best American Essays,* writes: "I'm not usually sold on epiphanies, especially of the life-transforming type. I'm more interested in the opposite experience: not those rare moments of startling insight or realization, but—what I suspect are more common—those sudden flashes of anxious confusion and bewilderment. I distinctly recall one of these reverse epiphanies (is there a word for these?) shortly after I began high school."

Rabbi Yaakov Leiner, whose teachings are gathered together in a book called *Beit Yaakov,* teaches that small annoyances should not be dismissed: "We must believe that in such times, when one has no inner peace—then most of all one's position is infinitely more profound and superior to the (times when the) intellect reigns. Indeed, God wishes, through them, to teach one new and holy lessons and appreciation of His ways." Even those experiences that seem annoying and insignificant may be filled with God. I can't help thinking about the coronavirus, a very big global annoyance and for many a tragedy. Yes, many of us who sheltered were annoyed and frustrated. But this time was also one of revelation: understanding what is really important to us, who we love and how we want our lives to be. Some people also discovered activities that they didn't have time for before—like drawing or prayer or meditation or listening to the birds. One day during the pandemic, I was doing dishes, rushing through them, and then I realized: I am in no hurry. I can enjoy this chore. This global annoyance and tragedy has given those of us who are well the gift of time.

◆

WRITING EXERCISE: ANNOYANCE AND CHALLENGE

- Write about something that bothers you, a moment of confusion or bewilderment, rupture or uncertainty. Let that moment inspire you.
- Write about the coronavirus. What was a particular challenge you

faced? One of my students wrote a beautiful essay about her corona-virus insomnia—the anxieties that woke her and plagued her (pun intended) at four in the morning.

⌐

Obstacles

Difficult emotions can inspire us to write, and yet sometimes we don't want to admit how resentful, jealous, or angry we feel. However, when a writer is willing to voice and explore darker feelings like fear, jealousy, humiliation, or anger that are not always shared in ordinary life, the reader may feel the great pleasure of intimacy, the confirmation of his own fears and shadows.

Less, the 2018 Pulitzer Prize–winning novel by Andrew Sean Greer, tells the story of a minor novelist's travels to writing events around the world to escape his former boyfriend's wedding. The narrator reveals a series of humiliations, but he leavens it with so much intelligence and humor that the reader can't help but take pleasure in the cascade of embarrassing and defeating encounters.

We may also resist inspiration because an inner voice says that we don't have permission to speak. Our narrative is dangerous. We suppress the story because we are afraid of revealing too much, harming others or ourselves, betraying even those who have hurt us. One needs to hold back and yet the story must be told.

"Art is confession; art is the secret told. But art is not only the desire to tell one's secret; it is the desire to tell it and hide it at the same time," wrote Thornton Wilder.

Sometimes we want to tell our secrets. Yet if our desire is vengeance, if we are motivated to get even with somebody, the reader may sense the narrator as bitter and untrustworthy.

Yet divulging secrets does not have to entail a complete confession. Confession, while titillating, can sometimes be degrading or melodra-matic. Writer Emily Fox Gordon distinguishes between a confession, which is blurted out to a person who has some power over us, and a confidence, which is written to a confidante or friend, creating an equal relationship. She explains that writing that confides, that whispers, that tells secrets without hurting others has the advantage of offering a stable narrator who invites the reader in. The narrator is not interested in exposing everything—showing the guest his dirty laundry and garbage—but in providing a relationship.

Privacy may be an outmoded term, but our privacy deserves respect. You can write a memoir without exposing family secrets, alluding to them without describing every detail—not because you can't tell the story but because you choose to respect your own dignity. Not everything needs to be told. The world is one where God is revealed and concealed at the same time. We may choose to do something similar in our work: expressing the emotions of our story while suppressing some of its secrets. Such essays may be even more powerful because the reader feels the undercurrents of pain in the gaps in the story. Writer Beth Kephart calls writers who don't divulge every detail artful dodgers, trusting the reader with "secret unsaids." You maintain the power of the emotion, the inner story, while playing with and transforming the outer circumstances.

It's a very hard balance, especially if you're a parent. There are many things I will not write about in a memoir because I don't want my children to read about them. I know this may be an unpopular position, but I find it necessary. Another option for keeping one's privacy is writing and sharing a story in a writing workshop with a small group of people who will keep your confidence. Sometimes my students say, "This piece is only for our class. And thank you for letting me trust you with this story." Yet another solution toward maintaining privacy is to transform elements of your story into fiction. In a novel I recently finished writing, the outer body of the story has very little to do with my life, while the inner struggles of the characters are close to my own. In other words, you can change "the dress" but keep the fire of the inner conflicts—"the body."

On the other hand, you may choose to tell the whole story because you need to and are willing to deal with the consequences. My friend, poet Jane Medved, got the following advice in a master class: if you're going to jeopardize a relationship, make sure that it is worth it. You better have a great piece of writing if you're going to take such a risk. Your relatives may be angry. An uncle may stop talking to you. A sister may write a competing memoir. Or your family may not even notice.

Writing Exercise: Shame and Anger

- Write about an experience where you felt a sense of shame. Shame is one of the most powerful forces in our lives. Tell the whole story. Next talk directly to somebody in the story. Tell him what you couldn't say then. Now talk to your shame. What do you want to say to it? Let the shame answer you. Use any of these sections in an essay.
- Anger can also serve as an inspiration. What makes you furious? Tell the reader and let it rip. Don't hold anything back.

A Few Methods of Inspiration

- Open a book and read a few sentences. Put your finger randomly on a sentence and see if that sentence speaks to you in some way. Respond to that sentence. When you are finished, you can flip the book open and find another word or sentence to use as a prompt.
- Eavesdrop. Make a list of ten phrases or sentences you overhear. Use one or many in an essay.
- Songs and scents are filled with strong associations, triggering the amygdala and the hippocampus, parts of the brain that spark emotion and memories. One of my former students, Stella, a widow in her seventies, wrote a wonderful essay inspired by a song called "Mambo 8" that she danced to when she was a teenager in London fifty years ago. At the time, she was fleeing the Jewish world of organized dances for the wild free atmosphere of a club. Write about a song or a scent. Or both.

- Write about somebody who inspired you. Who was she? What did she teach you? How do you incorporate her teaching into your life?
- Write about a role model who ultimately disappointed you. How did she inspire you at first? What happened to cause your disillusionment? Or perhaps the reverse happened: you were unimpressed with somebody and then learned to be inspired by her. Tell us what happened.
- Pick a sentence from the Torah or other spiritual text. Use that sentence as the epigraph or first sentence of your writing, or thread that sentence into your text when you are looking for inspiration. Repeat that sentence or variations of that sentence in your text.
- Write about something you unexpectedly found or received. Once when teaching a writing seminar for high school students, I found a blue diving flipper on the road in front of the school that morning and asked the students to write a story that included the flipper. That was their best work the whole semester.
- Let both an object and a word inspire you. Pick an object in the room where you sit. Describe the object in detail. What does it look like? Sound like? Feel like? Does it remind you of a story? Allow unexpected connections to happen on the page. Next open the dictionary and close your eyes and thumb through the pages. Put your finger on a word. Open your eyes. Let that word inspire you. (If that word doesn't resonate with you, pick another.) Play with the word. Enjoy it. Riff on it. Improvise. See if you can connect it to your writing about the object. Associations may be oblique yet surprising. Allow for serendipity.

The object Mayan writes about is a large papier-mâché sculpture of a giraffe perched on the ledge of the living room. The word she alights on is *inglenook*.

After describing the giraffe, Mayan writes about her brother who died recently in South Africa. She tells the story of how years earlier, they had gone on safari in the winter and seen giraffes. She remembered how they returned to the inglenook of his home and how warm and wonderful she felt with him there. The word *inglenook* provides a safe entrance into the strong feelings evoked by her brother and his death.

Ruth doesn't pick a word from the dictionary but responds to the puzzle that is framed on the wall in the house where we hold class. She uses the word *puzzle* as inspiration and writes about traveling on a subway in Toronto and how all at once a group of beautifully dressed young people entered the subway car. One of the men grabbed the metal subway pole and spun around on it in joy. The women were made up, perfumed, wearing gowns and high heels. Ruth was puzzled until she saw a photographer snapping photos of a bride and groom in wedding clothes at the other end of the car. They were all part of a wedding party, taking pre-wedding pictures on the subway. She framed the story around the fact that she was a widow, and the young people in the subway caused her to miss her husband and marriage and youth.

Writing Exercise: Finding Inspiration

- Let your name inspire you. In Jewish thought a name is a kind of prophecy. What do you like about your name? Dislike about it? Why did your parents give you the name? What do you know about your name? How popular was your name in the year you were born? Tell us everything you can about your name.
- It's true that you should write about what you know. But you can also write about what you would like to know. What topics are you interested in knowing more about? Yoga, geology, nuclear physics? These topics (and research) can inspire essays.
- What role has inspiration played in your life? Your work? Your relationships? Your travel? Your adventures? What have you learned about inspiration?
- What are quotations or sayings that inspire you? Make a list of

those sayings and keep them at your desk. Begin an essay with one of them.

- In the mid 1800s, Friedrich August Kekulé, a German chemist researching the structure of benzene, discovered its ringlike molecules only after he dreamed of a snake that was catching hold of its tail, inspiring him to envision the structure of the chemical. Write about a dream you had and let it inspire you. Let your unconscious speak to you. Explore a few possible interpretations.

- Listen to radio shows and podcasts where authors are interviewed about their work. I enjoy *Fresh Air,* an NPR show hosted by Terry Gross, and Krista Tippett's show *On Being.* You can also listen to great storytelling on podcasts, such as *Fiction Podcast,* presented by the *New Yorker* magazine, and *The Moth.* Rabbi Joey Rosenfeld has a wonderful podcast called *Inward,* where he explores the major works of Kabbalah and Jewish philosophy.

A Warning about Inspiration

Inspiration can dissipate if it is not translated into action. We all know plenty of people who are creative geniuses with amazing new ideas, yet they are unsuccessful because they never transfer their enthusiasm and inspiration into practical activity. Don't talk too much about your project. Write instead.

Another obstacle to inspiration is the writer's inability to finish anything. Obviously, writing requires not just inspiration but persistence (as we shall discuss in a later chapter). It's important to finish your work, even if it's not perfect. Once the imaginative process is complete, your experience and ideas expressed and transformed, you can leave them. Even if they aren't posted or published, the work is never wasted because it moves you to the next writing project. Use some of the "leftovers" in another text you write. Now your imagination is ready for new arrivals.

3
Comprehension
Bina

THE NEXT SEFIRA, *BINA* OR COMPREHENSION, is the step beyond inspiration that allows you to develop your initial ideas. While chochmah or inspiration contains enormous potential, bina provides a framework to structure the emerging story. Bina is related to the Hebrew word *boneh,* which means "to build." How do you advance your writing from one thought or image to the next and, perhaps, to a resolution? The word *comprehend* comes from the Latin *comprehendere,* which means to "seize or grasp." The narrator in your essay often journeys from confusion to clarity and understanding, grasping the significance of the material.

Bina is the process of intuiting one matter from another, the ability to weave a pattern, to discern a structure emerging from chaos and darkness. E. L. Doctorow describes it like this: "Writing is like driving at night in the fog. You can only see as far as your headlights, but you can make the whole trip that way."

As artists, an integral part of our work is revealing patterns and outcomes in our stories that seem inevitable but not predictable. In *The Four Quartets,* T. S. Eliot writes: "In my beginning is my end." By the end of the poem he tells us that "in my end is my beginning." *Sof ma'aseh, b'machshava techlila* are the words in a Hebrew song that is sung in prayer on Friday night, the Jewish Sabbath. The words mean "the end of the action is already latent in the beginning of the thought"—the two are intimately linked.

⌣· ·⌣

In *Pirkei Avot, the Ethics of the Fathers,* an ancient book of Jewish morality, Rabbi Yohanan ben Zakkai asks his five most distinguished disciples: "What is the most important character trait to live by?" According to the text, Rabbi Shimon's answer is the most satisfactory. He says, "*Ha'roeh et ha'nolad*"—the one who sees what will be born.

The ability to envision an outcome does not just entail reason but often demands patience and faith. We intuit the path of the text, sense its development, as if our text has a destiny. We discover a design in our work. However, that doesn't mean that the ending is a tidy solution. Sometimes the ending may be a further complication, a question.

The short-story writer Grace Paley says that a story is a circle that doesn't close but leads toward something else. It can glance back at where it started, but the closing can surprise both the reader and the writer.

In fact, complete closure or resolution may be a fiction because it implies that all things can be processed, resolved, and comprehended. There are many writers who refuse to search for an artificial resolution to their work, mostly because life rarely offers those neat endings. Daniel Mendelsohn, for example, says that his book *The Lost* was not a search for closure because so many of the people who died in the Holocaust died without any sense of completion:

> I set out to write an anti-closure search narrative, in which I foregrounded what I hadn't learned, haven't found out—the best way of reminding readers of a crucial ethical and historical point: that most of the Holocaust's victims and their stories were indeed lost.

I'm very uncomfortable with the concept of closure. There is no way I will ever be finished with my son's murder. Some things are so filled with horror and pain that they demand respect: our intellect will never be capable of resolving such heartache. We don't move on; we move with. There's an ongoing relationship with the person who died, rather than a complete separation.

Even in stories that are less fraught, we may not want to tie our story tight with a string or ribbon but instead may gently close it with a pinch, the way that the braids of challah dough are secured before baking. I've heard that action described as a kiss.

In this chapter we will look at how a Jewish model of hermeneutics, *pardes,* can help us develop our essays so that they are rich and textured.

The Garden and the Sages
A Pattern for Essay Development

The mystical pattern of pardes mentioned in the Zohar, a book of Jewish mysticism, offers a rich model for shaping, developing, and building our essays, memoirs, and stories. According to the story of the pardes, four sages entered the pardes or garden, but only one survived and emerged unscathed. Ben Zoma looked and went mad, Elisha ben Abuyah became a heretic, and Ben Azzai looked and died. Only Rabbi Akiva entered in peace and departed in peace, able to withstand the searing closeness of God's presence.

Pardes is the name of this mythical garden (related to the word *paradise*), but it is also an acronym for *pshat* (the simple meaning), *remez* (what it reminds us of), *drash* (the interpretation), and *sod* (the secret that waits to be revealed), four levels of hermeneutics or biblical interpretation. These four components provide a conceptual map for analyzing any experience or encounter. They also offer an excellent structure for enriching and developing our writing.

Detail
Pshat

Pshat, which translates as "the simple meaning," can be thought of as the concrete experience, the *whatness* of the situation, the telling details: the who, what, when, where. When we write, we conjure a world for our reader by describing the particulars of our experience. As Vladimir Nabokov says: "Caress the detail, the divine detail."

"The greatest writers," according to William Strunk and E. B. White, authors of the classic style manual *The Elements of Style,* "are effective largely because they deal in particulars." William Carlos Williams, a Pulitzer Prize–winning poet (and a doctor) from New Jersey, says: "No ideas but in things." Hemingway says: "Abstractions are the lies of a dying civilization."

Poet and memoir writer Mark Doty refers to description as the ability to pour into the now, submit to the moment, an immersion that offers us to access deeper perceptions. For example, in *Now Write! Nonfiction,* Celeste Fremon recounts that when mystery writer Michael Connelly worked as a crime beat reporter in Florida, one day he noticed the worn grooves in the temples of a detective's glasses. The detective put the glasses in his mouth and bit on them when he was working an investigation. That powerful detail revealed the detective's concentration as well as his anxiety. Robert Morgan, author of *Gap Creek,* a novel based on his grandparents' marriage and their hardscrabble life together, writes: "I tell my students that you do not write living fiction by attempting to transcribe actual events onto the page. You create a sense of real characters and a real story by putting down one vivid detail, one exact phrase at a time."

To evoke a world for our readers, we may begin by thinking about place. "For there is no person who has not his hour, and no thing that has not its place" (*Ethics of the Fathers,* chapter 4). I just spoke on the phone to a friend who is very ill, suffering from respiratory problems. She was taken from the hospital to a rehab center, and she told me anxiously that she doesn't know where she is. Knowing where we are is our first step in being present in the world.

Furthermore, it may be that in describing a place, we also in some small way help rescue it. The Kabbalah tells us that the world could not endure the overwhelming nature of God's light so the light shattered all over the world, and in each place it is our job to gather the shattered pieces. We can think of place not only as a background or setting but as a locus awaiting attention, concern, and even redemption.

As writers, we root the reader in a specific time. What is the month? The year, the hour? You can provide a setting for your reader in the very first sentences: *It's 10:03 on a Sunday morning, and I write from my office in Tekoa, which also functions as a guest room and a cheder maamad, a shelter in case of war. The room, built from reinforced concrete, has a heavy metal door that could close and trap me because the clunky metal door handle has fallen off.*

We create a scene, the essential building block of writing, by writing about concrete details. What is the light like? The weather outside? What do the people look like, the furniture? What are the sounds and sights and smells? What covers the windows? What is on the table? What color is the couch? What are people drinking? What is the headline of the newspaper that day? Small children are often admonished "not to make a scene." You have permission now to make a scene come alive by recording the telling details.

Significant details also help us describe a character. We can learn more, sometimes, by the way somebody stands or clenches their hands when they speak than from what they say. I'm reminded of the fact that in job interviews, a person is judged in the first fifteen seconds, and most of that is by the way he carries himself. When writing about a character, imagine that person. (When I'm in a café or other public space, I like to look at people so I can work on describing people's physical details, especially their faces.) What does her nose look like? His lips? What is the most obvious feature on the person's face or body?

What is he wearing? Are there stains on her clothes? What does she do with her hands? A telling physical detail can sometimes intimate the inner character of the person. Laurence Olivier said that to unlock a character he always started with the shoes.

Pshat allows concrete details to speak to us. What was in your father's pockets? What did he smell like? (Smell is the hardest sense to describe, and for that reason, it's often helpful to use a metaphor.) What did you eat for dinner and where and with whom? When you were a child, who woke you up in the morning? My father woke me up with a cup of coffee and the song, "Lazy Bones." However, don't think that when you describe something you should always amass a catalog of detail. It's important to select the details of pshat according to the mood, feeling, and theme you want to convey in your text. Description can be thought of as another character in the narrative, which shares in building the emotional tenor of the story.

—

WRITING EXERCISE: NOTICING DETAILS

According to the Baal Shem Tov, the great rabbi and founder of the Chassidic movement, everything we see and hear can be thought of as a message from God. By writing about these details, we respond to and appreciate God's nudges and hugs. Observing and describing in detail the ordinary can be the gateway to something deeper, even divine.

Describe your parents' kitchen or your own kitchen. Slow down time. Use all of your senses. The scene is like a close-up, a camera zooming in. Put yourself in that room.*

What is the hour, day, month, year?
Where is the scene set?
What do you see from the window?

---

*Adapted from "Your First Kitchen" by Robin Hemley in *Now Write! Nonfiction*.

What is the weather like?

What is the light like?

What objects and appliances are in the room? Their sizes and shapes?

How is it furnished?

What do you hear? What do you touch? What are the textures?

What is the smell? What does the smell remind you of?

Is the room tidy or untidy? Is there something unusual in the room?

What's on the walls?

Are there knickknacks around?

What is in the cupboards?

What is under the sink?

Is there a clock ticking? What does it look like?

What do the curtains look like?

In my mother's kitchen, old dried-out teabags lounged in a china cup over the sink because my mother liked weak tea and reused her teabags. A plywood plaque near the pantry closet had these words painted on it: Who's in the doghouse? Five dog medallions inscribed with the words *mom, pop, sis, sis, brother* hung from metal hooks, although we had no use for the brother medallion. Only one medallion could be hung in the doghouse at a time. My grandmother sat at the kitchen table, reading Agatha Christie mysteries and smoking Viceroys, her ashtray a yellow candy dish patterned with flowers, adorned with a silver handle.

WRITING EXERCISES: PROMPTS TO PRACTICE PSHAT
Particulars about People

Andre Dubus III offered this exercise at a writing conference I attended:

- Write about five people and describe them by their smells.
- Pick three of these people and describe them by the light around them.

- Pick two of these people and describe them by the sounds that you associate with them.
- Now choose one person and write a scene that includes many of these sensual details.

Food Narrative

- Write a narrative about food and include a recipe. Did anything weird, funny, or unusual happen to you while cooking, shopping, preparing a meal, or feeding your family or guests? You could also write about your mother's cooking, your child's cooking, any cooking or baking for that matter. Set the scene first. What does the table and the kitchen look like? Smell like? What's the lighting? Who is in the kitchen? What are people wearing?
- Thomas Lux wrote a magnificent poem called "Refrigerator, 1957." Write about a refrigerator from your childhood. Describe what was always in there or write about an item in it that symbolizes that era for you.

Large and Small

During a workshop at the Vermont College of Fine Arts, I heard memoir writer Kyoko Mori say that, of course, you can write about loss and trauma but don't torture your audience. And I would add, "Don't torture yourself." You can write about the death of a loved one by writing about something particular and concrete associated with the person. For example, write about her hair or the pipe he smoked, or the scarf she gave to you. Let the object carry the weight and burden of the emotion. Writer Ann Hood says that you can write about something small at the same time that you are writing about something enormous. Eventually, the two will merge.

⌁

Hint

Remez

Remez means "hint," as in textual connections and associations. Instead of writing a simple anecdote, investigate its greater significance. Did something similar happen to you years ago? What connects the two events? Does your story remind you of a scientific study you read about? A historical event? Don't be afraid to explore biology, history, chemistry, or physics to expand your narrative. Not only do you present interesting information but you also become a more reliable narrator, a fascinating tour guide, because you demonstrate your interest in the world by amassing knowledge and information that you share with others. In addition, the research often suggests meanings that you may not have even considered. As the poet Horace said about poetry, *educate and delight.*

Here is British author and naturalist Helen Macdonald writing about the migration of birds (from *H Is for Hawk*):

> Watching the cranes at dusk, I see them turn first into strings of musical notation, then mathematical patterns. The snaking lines synchronize so that each bird raises its wings a fraction before the one behind it, each moving flock suddenly resolving itself into a filmstrip showing a single bird stretched through time. It is an astonishing image that makes me blink in surprise. Part of the allure of flocking birds is their ability to provoke optical illusions. I remember my astonishment as a child watching thousands of shorebirds flying against a gray sky vanish and reappear in an instant as the birds turned their counter-shaded bodies in the air.

The birds remind the author of startling images—musical notation and mathematical patterns. They also evoke a memory from childhood, her astonishment at seeing shorebirds disappear and then appear again.

Here's another example from an essay in the *New York Times*

Magazine on bath oils where the writer, Molly Young, is reminded of a novel she read:

> A slug of liquid poured into the tub will release healthful vapors and stain the water brightly: orange, mauve, spruce, blue. Doing this brings to mind a line from Dodie Smith's novel "I Capture the Castle." In it, a character dips her handkerchief into a vat of fabric dye and observes: "It really makes one feel rather Godlike to turn things a different color."

Incorporate your memories into your essays. You add texture to the writing as you probe and explore the way that memories reverberate with events in the present.

Explanation
Drash

Drash literally means "to explicate and explain." What are the ideas you are grappling with in your work? These ideas become your themes—the core, the heart, the things that you as a writer have come to say. What haunts you? What arouses you? What upsets you? What frustrates you? What is your passion? Your obsession?

Your theme may not be stated explicitly, but you might want to state it for yourself: What is the question at the center of your text? What idea are you trying to get at? In *The 3 A.M. Epiphany: Uncommon Writing Exercises That Transform Your Fiction,* Brian Kiteley suggests that we are writing to learn, not to teach. In this way, as writers, we seek meaning, but we do not have to arrive at a definitive answer. In fact, our theme does not have to convey a moral message. Here is Mark Twain's wonderful warning in his introductory note to *The Adventures of Huckleberry Finn:* "Persons attempting to find a motive in this narrative will be prosecuted; persons attempting to find a moral in it will be banished; persons attempting to find a plot in it will be shot."

The writer is not concerned so much with didactic meaning but rather creative possibilities and patterns, offering the reader the possibility of gleaning meaning. As novelist John Gardner says: "Theme is not imposed on the story but evoked from within it—initially an intuitive but finally an intellectual act on the part of the writer" (from *The Art of Fiction*). The writer achieves clarity through the process of working on the story or essay.

Writing becomes an act of deep thinking that allows you to refine and clarify what it is you mean as you develop your thoughts. One image suggests another. An anecdote stirs a memory. As we transform anecdote into story, we find a pattern and meaning, what it is we are trying to get at. Yet we have to be careful of overexplaining. "To suggest is to create, to explain is to destroy," says the French poet Stéphane Mallarmé. In essays there's more room for the writer's interpretation on the page, but we should also be aware that readers want to participate in creating meaning. God left us with the need to complete the world he created, to make repairs where we find things lacking. Allow the reader to be part of the process of interpretation and completion.

Although we don't want to moralize, we also have to refrain from being a wishy-washy narrator. Writer and critic Phillip Lopate says that he has grown weary of students' essays that wander through a landscape without trying to say anything. He distinguishes between an essay that is an exploration and an essay that makes an argument and prefers a writer who is courageous enough to make a claim ("Exploration and Argument" in *To Show and Tell*).

Don't be afraid to assert a bold opinion. For example, in "Shooting an Elephant," George Orwell's classic story of his experience as a police officer in Burma where he felt forced to kill an elephant, the writer clearly states his thesis: "When the white man turns tyrant it is his own freedom that he destroys."

Sometimes the writer only reveals the theme at the end of the text. E. B. White's essay "Once More to the Lake" is an ebullient story of his return with his son to the lake in Maine he enjoyed as a child. He seems to return to his youth, enjoying the peace and beauty of the lake until the final startling image. His son is dressing to swim during a rainstorm and the writer concludes: "As he buckled the swollen belt, suddenly my groin felt the chill of death." The reader is startled by the invasion of mortality, the reversal of tone and feeling.

Similarly, the ending of James Wright's poem "Lying in a Hammock at William Duffy's Farm in Pine Island, Minnesota" causes us to reevaluate everything that precedes it. The poem begins with a bucolic scene:

> *Over my head, I see the bronze butterfly,*
> *Asleep on the black trunk,*
> *Blowing like a leaf in green shadow.*
> *Down the ravine behind the empty house . . .*

The reader is lulled into a tranquil picture of a perfect day in nature that suddenly explodes in the last line:

> *I lean back, as the evening darkens and comes on.*
> *A chicken hawk floats over, looking for home.*
> *I have wasted my life.*

The poem lands with a punch to the gut, prodding the reader to question everything that came before the last line.

Another technique for revealing meaning is contradiction. Writers who embrace both sides of an opposition often seem the most truthful (from Brenda Miller, "The Date"):

Despite all I've tried to learn in the years alone—about the worthiness of myself as an independent woman, about the intrinsic value of the present moment, about defining myself by my own terms, not by someone else—despite all this, I know that my well-being this moment depends on a man's hand knocking on the door.

What's stressed (because it comes at the end of the sentence) is the narrator's need for the man's arrival, but her strong desire for independence is also recognized. Both are true. The narrator does not shy away from complexity.

Here's another example from "Kentucky" by Lee Martin:

> I didn't understand, then, the complicated crosscurrents that run through a family's affections, though eventually I would figure out that even in my father's anger, and my anguish as a result of it, lay a wellspring of genuine love.

Martin's disabled father was violent, but the writer adds that this did not mean that his father didn't love him, a painful confession. The writer leads us to understand a terrible truth: love is sometimes built on explosive ground.

In *Essays after Eighty,* poet Donald Hall states: "Essays, like poems and stories and novels, marry heaven and hell. Contradiction is the cellular structure of life." Furthermore, Hall claims that if the essay doesn't include contraries, the essay fails: "The emotional intricacy and urgency of human life expresses itself most fiercely in contradiction. If any feeling makes a sunny interminable sky, the feeling is a lie and the sky is a lie."

When a writer is able to enter the complexity of a contradiction, he reveals the truth of life—meaning isn't a matter of polarity—either this or that—but exists between those two places. Every decision includes a shadow. Every love contains a degree of hatred, and every peace includes a hint of war.

—

WRITING EXERCISE:
COMPLICATIONS AND CONTRADICTIONS

Write about your first boyfriend or girlfriend—or a friendship—but include contradiction. What was puzzling or complicated about the relationship?

Perhaps what you first liked about the person later became a source of anxiety. How did this relationship influence other relationships?

⌣

Theme as a Container

Theme determines and circumscribes what material needs to be included in the text, according to the points that the writer is driving toward. The writer creates narrative momentum, and she needs to make sure that she doesn't include material that isn't relevant. There can be detours on the way, but they should be tied to the overall search for meaning.

Moreover, theme is crucial because most of us live our lives searching for meaning. What is the best way to live? Who do I love? To whom and what should I devote myself? Is there a God? Where do I find my truth? Drash confirms that we are creatures who continually seek meaning.

⌣

WRITING EXERCISE: ME AGAIN

Write about something that has been a constant theme in your life. Give specific examples and anecdotes that illustrate that theme. Is there a pattern that you can discern?

⌣

Reflection

To tease out the meanings in our text, revealing and developing themes, we engage in reflection. In fact, it's often the depth of reflection that creates a compelling essay. Anybody can have an experience, but it's the way we process experience—our generosity of spirit, our perceptions, our willingness to be vulnerable, our insights—that gives the memoir its power.

The source of the word *reflect* is the Latin *reflectere,* which means "to bend back": the ability to see what we can only see when we look behind us, in retrospect. Phrases like *I think, I feel, I wonder* allow us to create a narrator who looks back in time from a different perspective and questions, speculates, and investigates.

In seeking meaning, the writer may alternate between text that describes concrete details of scene and text that reflects on experience. There's a pause in the action, and the interior voice takes over. Think of the announcers in professional football: one reports the plays and one provides the color commentary, talking about the player's past, his injuries, his family life, the scandals he has been involved in.

As a writer, you do both. In this way, most writing doesn't just record what we saw and experienced; it also invites our most intimate thoughts and feelings. The landscape of consciousness is bound to the landscape of action. We muse (and amuse), meditate, comment, feel, contemplate, summarize, explain, interpret, evaluate, analyze, and imagine. We confess and we worry.

"The two selves are the experiencing self, which does the living, and the remembering self, which keeps score and makes the choices," says Daniel Kahneman, a Nobel Prize–winning economist and psychologist. Sue William Silverman, award-winning author of several memoirs, has another way of referring to these two selves: the innocent narrator and the experienced narrator. The innocent narrator lives the story, but it is only with the benefit of time that the experienced narrator can look at the past and find the meaning in her story—a wise woman.

Writer Jon Franklin explains that sometimes when his university students write about family members who are dying of cancer, they often believe that the diagnosis is the epiphany of the piece. He helps them to understand that the point of insight is more likely the patient's conquering of fear, his inner story, rather than the diagnosis of cancer. "By point of insight I mean the moment when the story turns toward the resolution, when the main character (and/or the reader) finally grasps the true nature of the problem and knows what must be done about it. There are fates we can't change, but we can deal with them in ways that allow us to retain our dignity and our sense of control." The narrator uncovers a truth that was not readily apparent.

In "Reflection and Retrospection: A Pedagogic Mystery Story," Phillip Lopate explains that this revelation of insight can be thought of as a gift:

> This second perspective, the author's retrospective employment of a more mature intelligence to interpret the past, is not merely an obligation but a privilege, an opportunity. In any autobiographical narrative, whether memoir or personal essay, the heart of the matter often shines through those passages where the writer analyzes the meaning of his or her experience. The quality of thinking, the depth of insight and the willingness to wrest as much understanding as the writer is humanly capable of arriving at—these are guarantees to the reader that a particular author's sensibility is trustworthy and simpatico.

Many people have interesting lives, but the essay writer is the person who can provide the reader with insight and awareness. With retrospective awareness, the essay writer enters the past and comments on it, questions it, finds meaning where there was none initially. What does the writer know now that he did not grasp then? You may notice that in memoir the narrator often states: "What I didn't understand then was . . ." or "What took me years to realize was . . ." This is the writer's mature understanding, a voice of wisdom.

In *Re-Authoring Lives: Interviews and Essays,* narrative therapist Michael White says that insight can be thought of as a therapeutic achievement: "Stories provide the frames that make it possible for us to interpret our experience, and these acts of interpretation are achievements that we take an active part in." In this way, each story is two stories, the ostensible outer story, which is like the garment of the story, and the inner story, which is the body, the deeper theme, the real story—the narrator's path of reckoning, understanding, and awareness.

In the Torah when Moses asked to see God, he could only see God

from behind—"and you will see my back but my face shall not be seen."
As we are living, events come too quickly and closely to process. But
with the benefit of time and consciousness, as we write, we can see our
lives from behind—and may even be worthy of divine revelation.

⸺

A Wise Narrator

Write about a disturbing or traumatic event. Tell us the story and describe
the emotions you experienced. What has changed in your understanding
of the event? What did you feel then and what do you feel and understand now? What had to happen for you to be able to see the experience
differently? Be a kind and wise narrator.

⸺

Techniques of Reflection That Foster Insight
Questions

My friend Dr. Deborah Risk Tobin, a therapist for forty years, told me
that when she meets with patients who are resistant and armored she
tries to find a way to get beyond the posturing, and what she always
finds is the hidden pain. How does she build this trust with her patients?
By asking questions. We all know people who never ask us questions
about anything we say. But those curious or empathetic people who do
question us (gently) often help us to clarify what we are thinking, what
we need and desire.

Rabbi Hutner said: "There is no good answer that does not come
from a question." Questions like *Could it be? How is it possible?* give
us the ability to examine, probe, and understand. In addition, phrases
of uncertainty like *perhaps* or *maybe* or *it might have been* or *I wonder
if* encourage us to speculate, to examine and discard hypotheses about
behavior and experience, imagining alternatives and possibilities,
appraising and reappraising, deepening the questions.

The four questions that are asked at the Passover Seder are a central device for sharing the intergenerational story of the Exodus, the

central story of the Jewish people. Socrates, of course, employed a system of disciplined questions to engage his students. The complexity of our thinking and analysis corresponds with the level of the questions that we ask.

Here is an excerpt from the memoir *Circling My Mother* by Mary Gordon that illustrates the power of asking questions, as the writer probes the dilemma of writing about the taboo subject of her mother's body.

> How is it possible to speak of a mother's body?
> Possible, that is, without betrayal?
> And if it is possible, is it permissible?
> To speak of it as if it were not a body but something
> that could be turned into a work of art?

Gordon wonders about the legitimacy of writing about her mother's body: Is it a betrayal or a topic that is permissible? Her questions allow the reader to understand both her courage and her hesitancy.

Barbara Kingsolver says that when writing a novel she always starts with questions that she can't answer: "Otherwise you get bored halfway through if you already know the answers. If you're asking what seem to be unanswerable questions, then you have to keep showing up." When you write, try to ask a question that you don't have the answer to and see what happens. Even if you don't find an answer, the exploration will be real.

Rainer Maria Rilke understood the importance of questions and cautions us not to be hasty in trying to answer questions before we are ready (from *Letters to a Young Poet*):

> Be patient toward all that is unsolved in your heart and try to love
> the questions themselves like locked rooms or like books written in
> a very foreign tongue. Do not now seek the answers, which cannot
> be given you because you would not be able to live them. . . . Live the
> questions now. Perhaps you will then gradually, without noticing it,
> live along some distant day into the answer.

I love that phrase: *Live the questions.* Don't come to hasty conclusions. Let yourself be confused, even in chaos, until an answer is slowly revealed to you.

In fact, it may be useful to envision your essay as grappling with a specific central question or line of inquiry. Sometimes the title of an essay tells the reader exactly what that question is, for example Carlos Fuentes's essay, "How I Started to Write," or Wole Soyinka's essay "Why Do I Fast?"

Repetition

Repetition is a form of reflection that enables us to slow down the narrative in order to seek meaning. We repeat words or sentences to make sense of experience and provide a sense of coherence in the essay.

We can think of repetition as a form of meditation, continuous calm thought on some subject, deep thinking, and reflection.

Repetition can also be thought of as ruminating, to chew something over and over. The writer attempts to digest his experience—to absorb it. In fact, the psychological act of rumination is linked to post-traumatic growth. Professor Richard Tedeschi from the University of North Carolina found that survivors of trauma who give themselves time to deal with big questions—such as *Why did I survive? Is there a God? What should I do with my life now?*—sometimes experience a leap in their creative powers. They re-vision their lives because they provide themselves with time to process and integrate their experience.

In addition, all repetition creates emphasis, as we circle and home in on what concerns us. In life when we find that events repeat themselves, it may be a sign to pay attention: the unconscious is trying to speak to us.

The repetition of language in a text can also create a sense of coherence and harmony. Think of a refrain in music: the melody advances and builds so that when we return to the refrain, it's the same and yet different. Each repetition can be thought of as an escalation—more like a spiral than a circle. The key in writing is to find ways to repeat without being repetitious, without being boring or monotonous.

An example of the cumulative power of repetition (Terry Tempest Williams, "Why I Write"):

I write to make peace with the things I cannot control. I write to create fabric in a world that often appears black and white. I write to discover. I write to uncover. I write to meet my ghosts. I write to begin a dialogue. I write to imagine things differently and in imagining things differently perhaps the world will change. I write to honor beauty. I write to correspond with my friends. I write as a daily act of improvisation. I write because it creates my composure. I write against power and for democracy. I write myself out of my nightmares and into my dreams. I write in a solitude born out of community. . .

‿

WRITING EXERCISE: WHY DO YOU WRITE?

Tell us why you write. Use Terry Tempest William's template, beginning each sentence with "I write to" or "I write because."

‿

Structuring an Essay through Questioning and Repetition

Look at the way that Joan Didion employs *repetition* and *questioning* to seek meaning in her husband's sudden death in *The Year of Magical Thinking*:

Why, if those were my images of death, did I remain so unable to accept the fact that he had died? Was it because I was failing to understand it as something that had happened to him? Was it because I was still understanding it as something that had happened to me?

Life changes fast.

Life changes in the instant.

You sit down to dinner and life as you know it ends.

The question of self-pity.

You see how early the question of self-pity entered the picture.

Here, besides questions and repetition, we have the additional technique of short choppy sentences that imitate the stunned thinking of the narrator. As readers, we participate in the narrator's struggle to understand the tragedy she is experiencing. The writer creates a feeling of immediacy and urgency.

Repetition can also provide the scaffolding for an entire essay. Also known as *anaphora,* repeating a strong opening phrase creates a pleasing sense of rhythm and cadence. Anaphora can be employed at the line level, "Get busy living or get busy dying," or the repetition can be threaded throughout successive lines, as in Ecclesiastes 3:1–8, "There is a time for everything, and a season for every activity under the heavens: A time to be born and a time to die, a time to plant and a time to uproot."

Brenda Miller uses anaphora to structure her essay "The Date." She begins her essay with the sentence: "A man I like is coming for dinner tonight." Then a few pages later she adds: "A man I like is coming to dinner, so I get out all of my cookbooks and choose and discard recipes as if trying on dresses." Four paragraphs later she writes: "A man I like is coming to dinner which means I need to do the laundry and wash the sheets, just in case."

Variations in the repetition add interest as well as a sense of coherence.

—

Writing Exercise: Home is Where I . . .

Write an essay beginning: "Home is where I . . . ." Return to that phrase numerous times during the essay.

—

Negation

Some ideas and experiences can't be described or understood by what they are, but rather by what they are not. What isn't. What wasn't. What will never be. Some experiences are truly unnameable, impenetrable.

As writers it may make sense to focus on the negative image, like a painter who makes use of the negative space surrounding the images he creates. Sometimes, as in the abstract paintings of Jackson Pollock, the empty space becomes as important as the positive. (I once visited Jackson Pollack's studio in East Hampton where we were told to put on the paper slippers available to us in a basket. The drippings on the floor were not to be disturbed. It wasn't only the negative space of the paintings that had acquired significance but the evidence of Pollack's process as well.)

Negation is also a profound way of summoning up content and material that may have been repressed yet is needed for us to make meaning of our lives. Freud says: "To deny something is to say: that is something I would rather repress. With the help of the symbol of negation, the thinking process frees itself from the limitations of repression and enriches itself with the subject matter without which it could not work efficiently." Negation provides access to uncomfortable, disturbing material that may hide in the subconscious, waiting for expression.

It's sometimes easier to write about what isn't than to write about what is.

Often, negation and repetition go hand in hand as the author seeks meaning by recounting both what can and cannot be spoken of (Jamaica Kincaid, *My Brother*):

He did unspeakable things then, at least he could not speak of them and I could not really speak of them to him. I could name to him the things he did, but he could not name to me the things he did. He stole from his mother (our mother, she was my own mother, too, but I was only in the process of placing another distance between us, I was not in the process of saying I know nothing of her, as I am doing now), he stole from his brothers; he would have stolen from me, too, but the things he could steal from me were not available to him: my possessions were stored on a continent far away from where he lived. He lied. He stole, he lied, and when I say he did unspeakable things, just what do I mean, for surely I know I have lied and once I stole stationery from an office in which I worked?

Kincaid's use of repetition, negation, and questions replicates the intricate and unspeakably difficult tangled web of family and family responsibility. With these techniques she distances herself from her brother who did unspeakable things, yet by the end of the essay, she implicates herself as well: she admits that she lied and also stole office stationery.

Here is a striking example of negation. In *Circling My Mother,* Mary Gordon tells us what she does not want to say, which is often the most powerful psychic material:

> I know there are a number of ways I don't want to talk. A number
> of ways I don't want to write. I don't want to pity myself for being
> a child born of a body such as my mother's. And I don't want to
> describe my mother's body. Not anymore. Not now. I did it once.
> But she was living then. Now she is dead.

Finally, we can even negate our negation as in this quote from Keith Gessen: "As for me, I wasn't really an idiot. But neither was I not an idiot." Or this: "I hadn't been yelling. I didn't think. But I hadn't not been yelling either."

Gessen's attempts to clarify and qualify demonstrate the imprecision of language. His use of negation, while playful, highlights the difficulty of trying to understand ourselves and to communicate that knowledge.

Negation can also be employed to provide the structure for an entire essay, as in this example.

> Until I danced at my daughter's wedding, I didn't know how com-
> plex joy could be. I didn't realize that I could soar in abandon,

dancing with family and friends, and at the end of the wedding wave sadly goodbye to my daughter who was leaving our family with her husband. I didn't grasp that a wedding was a goodbye party.

But recently, my daughter had her first baby. When I visited her in the hospital, the nurse asked if this was my first grandchild. I said yes. She answered: "Now you know joy!"

——

WRITING EXERCISES: REPETITION, QUESTIONS, NEGATION
Until I

Write an essay that begins: "Until I . . . , I did not know." Continue the essay with a sequence of sentences, such as: "I did not know," "I didn't realize," "I didn't grasp," and so on. Try to end the essay with a reversal—a positive statement like the one above: "Now you know joy!"

You can also write about a troubling experience and begin: "Until I [. . .], I did not know [. . .]."

Remembering and Not Remembering

I was fortunate to attend a workshop in Jerusalem with writer Brandel France de Bravo who gave us this exercise.

Think of an event that had great emotional gravity for you. Write a list of at least ten sentences that begin with "I remember." Then create another list with "I don't remember." Weave those sentences into an essay.

Three Events

Think of three things that happened in the past month that made an impression on you.* Why did you pick these events? Write about each event and then reflect on what they have in common. Use the techniques of repetition, questions, negation, and short choppy sentences to meditate, speculate, or hypothesize.

———————

*Adapted from "Three Things That Stopped Me in My Tracks" by Michael Steinberg in *Now Write! Nonfiction.*

First Memories

Think of one of the first memories you have of yourself a child. Where are you? Who is there with you? What's happening? Use repetition, questions, and negation to speculate on why you remember this and what this memory means to you.

⸺

Secret
Sod

The final level of pardes, *sod,* means "secret." Secrets are at the heart of many pieces of writing, since God, creation, the world itself, and even our own lives seem to be a secret. Every narrative is based on a question, a mystery, something we cannot understand. Mystery and secrets keep the reader in suspense, waiting for more information to be revealed. Secrets mirror the mystery of our lives, the inescapable mystery of death. The world is a mystery, yet as writers, we don't always have to solve that mystery; rather we need to respect it and honor it.

Sod is also connected to originality and creativity. What can you say that is uniquely yours? What can you say that stems from your unique vision and experience of the world? When you write a book proposal, the publisher wants you to look at the other books on the topic. Why is your book different? What do you have to say on this topic that hasn't been said before? When you are writing from your deepest most authentic self, you are capable of writing what nobody else has said because it is yours.

Sod is a surprise because it is distinct and original and authentic. What do you have to say that will surprise your readers (and yourself)? You may discover an *epiphany,* which literally means "the appearance of God." Each piece of writing has its own discovery. It may be your sudden understanding of the theme of the work or the way that the images work together. It may occur when you understand the deeper meaning behind the events you describe. It's that aha moment. And until you reach that moment of surprise, the work is probably not complete.

To summarize the pardes system of pshat, remez, drash, and sod: We paint a scene with vivid details, and then we remember a similar experience or reference a related text or scientific finding. We build our essay as we search for meaning through the act of reflection and may receive the gift of an epiphany or revelation, a secret that is revealed to us—a hint of the divine.

KINDNESS
Chesed

WE MOVE NOW FROM THE SEFIROT OF WILL, inspiration, and comprehension, which are considered cognitive intellectual qualities, to the next seven sefirot, which are regarded as more emotional. These seven scfirot correspond to biblical figures like Abraham, Moses, Joseph, and King David.

The first of the emotional sefirot, *chesed* or kindness, can be thought of as an expansive act of generosity, compassion, and unrestricted love, with properties that are similar to light. As Rabbi Aryeh Kaplan says in his book *Inner Space: Introduction to Kabbalah, Meditation and Prophecy:* "The main property of light is that it has no boundaries—it enters and penetrates without borders, indiscriminately."

When we write, chesed enhances our generosity of expression so that we don't hold back or save anything. We aren't miserly with our words or our experiences. We let it all out without judgment.

Chesed corresponds to the biblical hero Abraham, who was able to give lavishly and freely. After his circumcision at the age of ninety-nine, even though he was in great pain, he stood outside his tent to welcome guests. When three travelers passed by his tent, he served them a feast. God waited while Abraham served his guests: we learn from this that hospitality to wayfarers is greater than welcoming the presence of God (Shabbat 127a). The biblical commentator Rashi states that the three men were angels who later informed Abraham that his wife, Sara, would have a baby (at the age of ninety). Sometimes kindness creates miracles.

Kindness, this radical generosity, is a way of saying yes, amen to the world. It reminds me of the art of improvisation. Butch Bradley, a comedian from LA, told me this about improvisation: *you say yes to everything.* Blue balloon, yes, Old City, yes, child sucking a lollypop, yes, pencil falling on the floor, yes, cell phone ringing in the middle of the show. Yes.

The more the better. Use it all. Think of what Nora Ephron's mother said to her and her sisters when they complained about their problems: *everything is copy.*

Yet there is a danger in too much chesed, too much love. For the first draft kindness is crucial in opening the channels of expression. But later, kindness can become a problem. For example, if a writer grows too attached to his material, he will not be able to cut what needs to be let go of. "You must kill your darlings" is a well-known writing maxim attributed to Faulkner. That which is overly beloved is sometimes sentimental or cliché. Language can be too pretty or literary. Elmore Leonard says that he cuts any sentence that sounds like writing.

In addition, kindness has to be used correctly and in its right measure. The sages say that he who is kind to the cruel will be cruel to the kind. Some commentators say that Abraham faced the greatest trial of his life when he was called upon to sacrifice his son Isaac precisely because Abraham embodied too much chesed and had to learn to restrict himself, to create limits and borders. Ultimately, he was not forced to sacrifice his child: God told him to take a ram as an offering instead of his son.

In this chapter we'll learn about the power of kindness: the importance of a generous first draft, the power of free writing, and how finding the right imagery can heal us.

Chesed also means that we are kind to ourselves as writers, taking our-selves seriously, giving ourselves time to devote to writing and editing: we carve out work time for ourselves, even if it's only a few hours a week.

Kindness in the form of self-compassion is crucial because it may enable us to keep working. Here's Elizabeth Gilbert on an important connection between kindness to ourselves and writing:

> As for discipline—it's important, but sort of over-rated. The more important virtue for a writer, I believe, is self-forgiveness. Because your writing will always disappoint you. Your laziness will always disappoint you. You will make vows: "I'm going to write for an hour every day," and then you won't do it. You will think: "I suck, I'm such a failure. I'm washed-up." Continuing to write after that heart-ache of disappointment doesn't take only discipline, but also self-forgiveness (which comes from a place of kind and encouraging and motherly love).

A Chassidic story underscores this link between love and discipline. A father was having terrible problems because his child refused to listen to him. The father asked his rabbi what he should do, expecting the rabbi to tell him to punish his son or at least reprimand him. Instead the rabbi said: *love him even more.*

The Blank Page and Kindness

When we write we may unconsciously imagine a reader who loves us—and whom we love. The essayist Phillip Lopate says that we create in our writing an ideal relationship with the reader, who we somehow believe will be our kind, patient mother. The blank page is supremely accepting and forgiving. For this reason, some of us are willing to write things that we would be reluctant to say to anybody in private.

The act of writing itself can also be thought of as a kindness because it is restorative. When we write we produce brain waves that are restful. Sometimes when I return to writing, especially if I have been away on a speaking tour, I feel my mind relax as I return to the empty page. Writing focuses our scattered thoughts and relaxes our brains. My creative writing professor, poet Archie Ammons, told me that even though he had won a Pulitzer Prize and many other honors, more important to him was the gift of the act of writing. Writing, he said, was its own reward.

Free Writing

Free writing is a generosity of expression, a means of creating flow that corresponds to the sefira of kindness. You write without judging yourself, without criticizing, without thinking too much, without going back, without erasing. You keep writing and open yourself to divine inspiration.

Set a time limit, for example fifteen minutes, and write. Let it all out. You don't have to correct yourself because everything is the way it needs to be. Whatever comes is what needs to be said. My yoga teacher sometimes says: "Let the breath breathe you." When free writing *let the voice speak through you.*

Trust the process. Allow digression, chaos, and a lack of control. You don't have to cross out or edit or censor: there's time for that later. Writer Marilynne Robinson tells us that in this stage, you're immersing yourself in the writing, connecting to your deeper mind, collecting material from your subconscious ("The Deep Mind: A Profile of Marilynne Robinson" in *Poets & Writers,* 2015).

Natalie Goldberg refers to free writing as first thoughts, those that aren't censored or edited. Buddhists believe that these thoughts contain tremendous energy because they are unmediated, closer to the divine source. In addition, with free writing, you can bypass those less-than-loving voices that tell you that you have nothing to say. Sometimes you are rewarded with insights that are discovered on the crooked paths of inquiry. When the Israelites left Egypt, God took them on a round-about path because he realized that if the people were close to Egypt, they would be afraid and would want to return to what they knew—even slavery. It's hard to leave the known world, no matter how awful it is. Free writing with its elaborate twists and leaps gives us the possibility of turning toward the unknown, the unconscious.

Make sure to save these pages because they can become first drafts. They have an energy, power, and truth that you will probably want to return to.

WRITING EXERCISE: FREE WRITING

Free write for ten days in a row, fifteen minutes a day. Do not censor. Do not erase. Do not go back. Just keep going. Peter Elbow, a pioneer in this process, says that if you feel that you have nothing to say, keep your fingers or pen or pencil moving and write "I don't know what to write" over and over until a thought comes to you. After you're finished keep whatever has energy. You may decide to develop the free writing into an essay or story. Or you may decide to leave it and start again tomorrow.

The Essay as a Form of Kindness

The personal essay is characterized by a generosity of form. Sara Levine in "The Essayist Is Sorry for Your Loss" describes essay writing:

> The essay seems disorganized. I think, because it has a stake in pretending not to know where it is going. Putting on its hat, heading for the door, it seems to follow the random movement of the mind itself. This looks like laziness but it smells like epistemology. Because essays offer a way of thinking, a dramatization of process as opposed to a curtain unfurled on the final product all scrubbed and clean as the newborn on TV.

As narrators, we are like tour guides, thinking aloud as we travel, allowing for interesting detours.

In addition, the essay embraces freedom as we gather the disparate and the discarded, that which sometimes arrives indiscriminately.

Part of the magic of the essay is the way that (in words poached from Walt Whitman) the form can contain a multitude: story, poetry, research, and stray bits of information can be collected and woven together. In this way, we are alert to a magic in living. When we are on the lookout for material, everything becomes more interesting.

The Loving Narrator

Readers may not respond to a narrator who indulges too much in self-pity or unjustified anger. Most readers identify with a narrator who, though she may have issues, insecurities, and idiosyncrasies, is ultimately tender, loving, and forgiving. For example, in this excerpt from *What Comes Next and How to Like It,* Abigail Thomas presents herself as a complicated, interesting, and likeable narrator. Also notice how she writes about herself in the third person, which gives her the narrative distance to step out of her personal angst.

> She used to think she needed to know things to be the mother. . . . But one weekend when her oldest daughter was afraid she was losing her baby, she spoke to her son-in-law on the telephone. Shyly, she asked him, "Do you think I should come?"
>
> "My wife needs her mother," said her son-in-law and in that second she understood all at once and forever everything she needed to know.

The narrator is down to earth, human, candid, imperfect, and loving. Like most of us. And the third person gives the reader the emotional distance to observe the narrator as she is observing herself. Elissa Schappell reviewed the book in *Vanity Fair* with these words:

"Irreverent, wise, and boundlessly generous." Wouldn't you love to have your book reviewed with those words?

In this excerpt from the essay called "Loitering" in *The Book of Delights,* Ross Gay also creates a generous narrator who seems to be very good company, even when he is speaking of a difficult topic:

> The Webster's definition of loiter reads thus: "to stand or wait around idly without apparent purpose" . . .
>
> Among the synonyms for this behavior are linger, loaf, laze, lounge, lollygaggle, dawdle . . .
>
> All of these words to me imply having a nice day. . . . Which leads to being, even if only temporarily, nonconsumptive, and this is a crime in America, and more explicitly criminal depending upon any number of quickly apprehended visual cues.
>
> For instance, the darker your skin, the more likely you are to be "loitering." Though a Patagonia jacket could do some work to disrupt that perception.
>
> A Patagonia jacket, colorful pants, Tretorn sneakers with short socks, an Ivy League ball cap, and a thick book that is not the Bible and you're almost golden. *Almost.*

Gay casts an eye on the pain and anger of feeling under attack because of his skin color yet his tone is almost playful. His critical yet loving stance toward the world allows the reader to feel both his pain and his joy.

Healing through Writing

Writing can also provide us with a means of healing from hurt and trauma. Though many of us are familiar with writers who suffered from mental illness, alcoholism, or depression and killed themselves, like Ernest Hemingway, Sylvia Plath, Anne Sexton, or David Foster Wallace, writing can also be a means of recovery.

Writing can offer us a modicum of control even in the midst of great chaos. For example, Joyce Carol Oates discusses the impulse to understand life through writing:

> The act of writing is an act of attempted comprehension, and, in a childlike way, control; we are so baffled and exhausted by what has happened, we want to imagine that giving words to the unspeakable will make it somehow our own. ("Why We Write about Grief," *New York Times*)

By translating our experience into a story, we give our pain a form, attempting to tame the traumatic experience. Even if that control is illusory, we find coherence in the chaos.

Meghan O'Rourke, a writer for the *New Yorker* and author of *The Long Goodbye* about her mother's death from cancer, says: "You know, writing has always been the way I make sense of the world. It's a kind of stay against dread, and chaos" ("Why We Write about Grief," *New York Times*). "If I told the story of her death, I might understand it better, make sense of it—perhaps even change it. . . . If I could find the right turning point in the narrative, then maybe, like Orpheus, I could bring the one I sought back from the dead. *Aha: Here she is, walking behind me*" ("Story's End," *New Yorker*).

I understand that need to keep a person alive by writing him alive. A few months after my son's murder, I began to write our story, Koby's story, about the mystical signs and experiences that occurred before and after his murder. Sometimes I felt like Scheherazade, the Persian queen who, under threat of death, told the king a story for a thousand and one nights: if I stopped writing, the pain would kill me.

I wrote in the hope of somehow keeping my son alive, but also because I needed a place to put my suffering. It's not that the pain went away, but I had something to contain it as I wrote, somewhere to release it for a few hours. I could hear my son's voice in my mind as I wrote and cried. Eventually, I crafted the story into a spiritual memoir, *The*

Blessing of a Broken Heart. My friend Ruchama King Feuerman, author of the novel *Seven Blessings,* says that there's a French word for this type of writing: *chantpleure.* To sing and cry together.

I'm drawn to the redemptive side of writing because I am trained as a certified pastoral counselor and run groups for bereaved mothers. Also over the years, I have met many people in my writing classes who have difficult and even tragic stories and yet, through writing, they experience breakthroughs—spiritual growth. I've had some students tell me that our writing class is better than therapy and much less expensive. John Freeman, the editor of the literary journal *Granta,* says: "It's easy to forget that prose can be a vessel for something which is broken; that a story can be the only thing you survive with." Prose is able to contain our rage, pain, and, ultimately, our love.

The author Michael Crichton is often cited as saying, "Writing is how you make the experience your own, how you explore what it means to you, how you come to possess it, and ultimately release it." (I will never release the sorrow of my son's murder, but writing has helped me live with it.)

Professor James Pennebaker of the University of Texas, a social psychologist, confirms that writing can benefit your health. In the 1990s Pennebaker researched the question: Why do people with terrible secrets often have health problems? He wondered: If people could share those secrets, would their health problems improve?

Pennebaker asked students to free write for twenty minutes for four consecutive days about an emotional upheaval in their lives. When students described the distressing incident in detail as well as the feelings they had about what had happened, their physical health improved. They had fewer visits to the health clinic, and their blood pressure was lower. But just writing about the distressing event itself did not elicit healing, nor did only venting feelings. The writer had to connect both the event and his emotions. In other words, the students had to narrate the pshat— the who, what, when, where, why—as well as the remez and drash, to reflect and comment on and interpret the meaning of their experience.

Changing the Past

When we write we have the unique opportunity to revisit and even revise that which hurt us. Debra Magpie Earling wrote the book *Perma Red,* based on the story of her aunt who died at the age of twenty-three, battered on the side of the road. Earling writes: "The wonderful thing about writing is that maybe we can avenge the dead." It's not that the past is changed, but we change our relationship to the past.

Writing offers us the generous possibility of accessing additional meanings that were not possible at the time of the experience. French philosopher Gaston Bachelard argues that there is a constitutive imagination, activated by reverie. *Reverie*—daydreaming or play with the symbolic imagination—is distinct from memory, which reflects on what has gone before and is dependent on and even stuck in the past. The dream like constitutive imagination has the power to affect and even change the past because the new imagery can reverberate with the events and experiences of the past and generate new material. In this way, alternative story lines and new meanings are fashioned. There's the possibility of imaginative release from the past. We write our way into an expanded future.

Literary Reality

Grammar itself offers a mechanism for creating a literary reality that transcends our lived experience. Conditional expressions in the past, present, or future voice what may not be possible in reality but is possible in language, and these possibilities create their own reality.

Subjunctive forms of verbs are typically used to express a hypothetical state such as a wish, desire, or imaginary situation. *If I were a butterfly, I would fly away.*

We describe a counterfactual reality, unbound by the rules of this world. For example, we state what we would have done or what we would like to do, regardless of whether or not we can actually do it. *I would like to be a nightingale singing in a forest. I wish I were six feet tall and could sink jump shots.*

These expressions give us the opportunity to voice alternatives:

> If I had been thinking, I would have said
> How I would have liked to
> I might have said
> I would have preferred
> I imagine
> Suppose?
> What if?

You can return to a scene and replay it, imagining a different or more satisfactory encounter or outcome—in the language of psychodrama, a kinder, preferred story, a surplus reality that exists in imagination.

Emily Hiestand employs counterfactual reality at the end of her essay "Hose." When she was a child, one afternoon, as her neighbor Mrs. Bayliss walked by her home, Emily and her brother turned a hose on her, not once but three times. In this excerpt the narrator, now a woman in her fifties, revisits her home and finds that Mrs. Bayliss has died:

> How I would like to have visited her once more, or to have taken our chances on a walk together down the hill to Jackson Square. Could I have found a way to thank her? It would have been a delicate undertaking, involving the risk of appearing completely unreconstructed. But I might have tried, for by her person, by her profoundly misplaced trust, the lady, Mrs. Bayliss, provided me a singular and pristine happiness—undimmed across five long decades.

The narrator doesn't seek forgiveness for her behavior during childhood. Instead, she wants to thank Mrs. Bayliss for that startling act of happiness. She can't thank her in person, but she does get to thank Mrs. Bayliss on the page, which creates a literary reality liberated from the constraints of the past. This literary reality, using words that are not possible to say in person, has its own expansive generosity and truth.

In the essay "A Bottle of Water in Brazzaville," Laird Hunt uses the mode of the counterfactual to describe his desire for a different outcome than the one that occurred when he was a visiting writing teacher in the Republic of Congo on behalf of the State Department. He enjoyed teaching his workshop on memory and imagination to these students who had recently endured a horrific civil war. At the end of the class, when Hunt was ready to board the van to take him back to his hotel, one of the students said he was thirsty, and the facilitator, himself Congolese, told the student to go back inside, suggesting that he'd find a bottle of water in the hot classroom. Laird and the facilitator both held bottles of water on that impossibly hot day, and Laird knew that there was probably no water awaiting his student who, no doubt, would have to walk many miles to return to his home.

> What I repeatedly find I cannot express, when I launch my verbal shards of that day into the air, in such poor imitation of my grandmother, is what I really mean to, the core of what I want to say about the moment. Which is something along the lines of, "One hot day in another country, I had some water and someone else was thirsty and I did not give him what I so easily could have." Which itself is a circumlocution, possibly an unforgivable one, for what I will never be able to say in person: "I'm sorry."

Though the narrator confesses that he will never be able to apologize in person, this apology, while imperfect and not directed at the right audience, is an admission of guilt that allows the writer to take responsibility for his mistake and imagine a different outcome. Though he could not offer kindness to his student, the writing allows him to imagine being a person who could and might if a similar situation were to arise. These words offer the author the possibility of change—and a hope of forgiveness.

Here is another example of counterfactual reality from *Hands* by Ted Kooser: a narrator voicing his desire to be embraced by his father. Though the narrator's father is dead, and can no longer hug him, the writing itself seems like an embrace.

> I would like to be held by these hands, held by them as they were when I was a child and I seemed to fall within them wherever I might turn. I would like to feel them warm and broad against my back and would like to be pressed to the breast of this man with his faint perfume of aftershave, with the tiny brown moles on his neck, with the knot of his necktie slightly darkened by perspiration.

In a more lighthearted way, wishes can allow us to engage in fantasy—a form of unbounded reality—as Nora Ephron does in her essay "Serial Monogamy" in *I Feel Bad about My Neck: And Other Thoughts on Being a Woman:*

> I always secretly wished that Lee [Lum] would include one of my recipes in one of his cookbooks—he frequently came to dinner and was always fantastically complimentary about the food—but he never asked me for any of my recipes.

She also fantasizes about imaginary conversations:

> I have always had a weakness for iceberg lettuce with Roquefort dressing, and that's one of the things I used to have imaginary arguments with Craig [Claiborne] about.

Writing can be a means for us to transcend the boundaries of our life so that we forgive, reimagine, and even reconstitute ourselves. In this way, memoir isn't just about the past. It's also about the future.

WRITING EXERCISES: LITERARY REALITY

- Write an essay that begins with *I would like* or *I wish*. Or take a story or essay you have written and change the ending so that it employs counterfactual statements like *I wish* or *I want to* or *if only* or *suppose* or *I imagine* or *I might have.*

- Write about something you meant to say, or wished that you had said. Somewhere in the essay state: *What I didn't say* (and wish I could have said). You can repeat that phrase as much as you want to. Tell us the story and reflect on the experience. In this essay you have the chance to reimagine your experience.

- Write an essay where you include a fantasy: cooking the perfect meal, speaking to your favorite writer, acting in a series on Netflix.

- Write an essay or a poem where each sentence or line begins with "I wish."*

- Write a few paragraphs where you imagine a whole other life for your mother or father or yourself. For example: "In my mother's other life, she is a singer in a jazz band and is applauded every night." Continue on with writing the fantasy life and see where it leads you.

---

*Adapted from an exercise in *Wishes, Lies and Dreams* by Kenneth Koch.

How the Fitting Image Heals Us

An image is something that you can see, feel, taste, touch, hear, or sense. The cup of old cold coffee with the skin of milk that looks like a map of France sitting next to your computer in the chipped "Happy Birthday" mug. The photo on the wall of your mother as a teenager standing next to an old black Ford. She's wearing blue overalls, her hair is in waves down to her shoulders, and a Pall Mall cigarette dangles from her mouth.

An image is alive, emotional. It carries a suitcase of meaning waiting to be unpacked. The young woman in the overalls, my mother, projects a feeling of freedom, all possibilities are open to the beautiful young woman.

Artist and writer Linda Barry says that images from childhood can conjure whole worlds. Even something as fleeting as a telephone number can offer us entrance into memory. (This may not work for those of you who grew up with cell phones and never had to memorize phone numbers!) When I think of my childhood phone number, I remember being a teenager, standing in the kitchen holding the yellow phone with its curly macaroni line, walking around the room until the cord stopped me as I talked to my friend Jan while waiting for the call interruption signal from a boy who I thought might finally call me.

Images offer complexity because they contain more than one symbolic meaning. There is no instant correlation, no one solution for an image. In a short video I saw recently in a gallery in Tel Aviv, a woman stood on the sand near a beach, surrounded by low thorny bushes. She wouldn't move from her place no matter who—whether an older man or a young woman—offered a hand, trying to help her. That image of being stuck conveys different meanings to different people: stubbornness or will, certainty or insanity.

But images do more than add dimension to our texts—they also offer us healing. Lynda Barry writes about V. S. Ramachandran, an innovative neuroscientist. He treated an amputee who suffered terrible pain because he felt that he constantly held his missing left hand in a tight fist that he couldn't release. Ramachandran had the patient insert his right hand into a mirror box and position it so he was tricked into seeing his left hand as if it were still part of his body. As a result, the patient could finally unclench his missing hand, and his pain went away.

Barry says that we all have losses, the loss of parents or friends or lovers. "The only way to open your fist," she says, "is to see your own trouble reflected in an image, a story, a poem, or a book you read." In other words, when we write or read, we may stumble upon or find images that mirror our own troubles, resonating with some deep emotional chord inside us, allowing us release from our pain.

I can attest to the power of imagery to effect healing. My first memoir, *The Blessing of a Broken Heart,* had no narrative design; it was a series of stories. But I realized that there were two images in the book that kept repeating: the cave and the bird's nest. My son Koby was murdered in a cave a quarter mile from our home. The year after Koby's murder, I experienced a series of mysterious encounters with birds: birds fell dead at my feet or hit the windshield of my car. A bird smacked against my head when I was walking on the beach. I dreamed about birds' nests.

Eventually, I understood that the images of the cave and the bird's nest could provide a narrative arc for the book. The cave, dark and closed, a place of sadness and darkness and terrible fear, contrasted with its reverse image, the bird's nest, which is open and a place of comfort and growth and nurturing. The nest became the narrator's aspiration— a movement away from the darkness of the cave toward air and light and birth and freedom. In addition, the bird's nest became an important signifier of theme: in the Kabbalah, it is written that the Messiah waits in the celestial "bird's nest" of the Garden of Eden to redeem the world. I was able to frame our family's tragic story as part of a larger story. It doesn't mean that by writing the book, I left my pain behind. But I did find a way to temporarily contain it.

The writer Isak Dinesen says that *there is no sorrow that can't be borne with a story.* Finding the right frame and imagery and language and narrative voice helps us bear our difficult stories. But there is another dimension to healing. One must also find the right audience. It's not just telling the story but the way the story is received and responded to that can provide additional healing. For example, one of my students wrote an essay about being alone with her mother when she died almost fifty years ago in a Jerusalem hospital. Rebecca, who was then nineteen, was visiting Israel with her mother, a widow. Rebecca and her mother were both first-time tourists to Israel, and when Rebecca's mother fell ill, Rebecca was totally alone in a foreign hospital, helpless in a society and language that were not her own. Many years later, in a chance encounter, a rabbi who had been in the hallway of the hospital the night that Rebecca's mother died told Rebecca that he had heard her cry of pain. He said, "I never heard anybody scream like that in my life." In class, Rebecca said that she realized that he had validated her suffering, which she thought had gone unwitnessed. Because of that recognition, the fact that her pain was acknowledged by another, a bit of her pain eased.

Another example: My student Stella's husband was one of the first heart transplant recipients in England. She wrote about leaving him in the hospital after his operation because she had small children at home and had to care for them. She tried to visit him the next day, but the nurses wouldn't let her in to see him. The next day, he fell into a coma, and he died before she saw him again. She wrote about her guilt in not being with her husband when he died, the painful feeling that she had abandoned him.

In class, one of the other students told her that often a person cannot let go and die when his loved ones surround him, and it could be that she had been kind to leave him. She was in her seventies by then and had never before thought of her husband's death without guilt.

Writing Exercises: Expansion and Transformation
Childhood Image

Write about a difficult incident you experienced as a child. Take an image from the story—something that you saw or heard or tasted or touched.

Now try to look at that image in a new way. Turn it inside out. Reverse it. Stand it on its head. A window can become a door. A circle can become a hula hoop. The glass holder for a *yahrzeit* candle* becomes a drinking glass (as it sometimes does).

What does the image tell you that you didn't know before? Let the image speak to you. Now talk back to that image. Incorporate some of this playfulness and reverie in the final text.

---

*A twenty-four-hour candle lit on the anniversary of the death of a loved one.

An Image and a Conversation

Structure an essay around an image and a conversation.* Images can serve as bookends for a scene. Place your characters in a specific setting and include an image, perhaps of a person's hands. Two people can have a conversation, disagree, or take some sort of action.

Now return to the image, which should be different in some way. For example, you could start with a woman stirring soup, wearing an apron. Two of her children sit at the table arguing about their father. At the end of the essay, the woman may do something different with her hands. The apron may be used to wipe up a spill on the ground. Or to wave out a small fire. Or be thrown in the garbage. Play with this, experiment.

An Apology

- Write an apology that you wish you had received from somebody.
- Now write an apology to somebody. Address the apology to a particular person. What did you intend and how did those intentions go awry? If you want, you can begin each sentence with "I'm sorry that . . ."
- Write an apology to yourself, a letter of forgiveness. Be kind and compassionate to yourself.

One Sentence

Write a page that is one long sentence, a run-on sentence. Be generous and expansive in language. Write about who and what you love, right now. Don't stop.

---

*Adapted from "Creating Shape in Scene" by Patricia Foster in *Now Write! Nonfiction*.

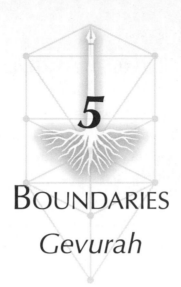

5

BOUNDARIES
Gevurah

GEVURAH MEANS LIMITS AND BOUNDARIES, an act of restriction. Rabbi Kook, the first chief rabbi of Israel, writes that only through constriction can the world take on a character that is seemingly independent of God. Otherwise, God would fill all available space, and there would be no room for anything except God. In addition, the world was created with boundaries, between the earth and the firmament, between the days of the week and Shabbat, between the ocean and the land.

Gevurah entails judgment, discernment, and discretion. It's not the opposite of kindness but complements it because gevurah concerns itself with giving what the other can receive. Thus, gevurah and chesed are always in relationship. Gevurah provides a container for kindness and love to protect these energies from being wasted or lost. It sets margins and limits. *Chesed* and gevurah are often depicted as hands that can embrace, carry, and contain. Chesed is the right hand, gevurah the left: love requires both.

The ability to contract, to hold back, is associated with the biblical figure Isaac who allowed himself to be bound for a burnt offering. When Abraham was called upon to offer Isaac as a sacrifice, Isaac resisted fleeing even though some sources say he was thirty-seven years old at the time. Isaac was able to limit his own needs, to restrain himself, even in the face of impending death. His father did not divulge his mission, but many commentators state that Isaac must have known. Isaac's gevurah was as powerful as his father's chesed and love for God. Still, Isaac paid a price for this act of devotion. A midrash* says that Isaac became blind in later years because the angels cried, and their tears fell into his eyes when he was brought up as a sacrifice.

Though gevurah may seem to be a less attractive quality than kindness, it's sometimes more valuable. For one thing, gevurah often has more staying power than chesed. A midrash tells us that Abraham had many followers who converted to his belief in one God, but as soon as he died, they reverted to idol worship. Isaac influenced fewer people, but they were able to integrate his teachings into their lives and continue the tradition of monotheism.

As writers, gevurah is crucial because it provides you with the ability to concentrate, to pay attention and move slowly and deliberately, to focus and linger if necessary. It is the ability to spotlight what is significant and delete the extraneous and to know the difference between the two. You are able to restrain yourself in order to achieve coherence. What you leave out in your work is as important as what you keep in. "Writing is not the main thing, but erasing," says Rev. Menachem Mendel Morgensztern of Kotzk, Poland, better known as the Kotzker Rabbi, who lived in the early nineteenth century. Michelangelo said that sculpture was cutting away until the essence was revealed. Gevurah, finding the boundaries of our work, brings us to the essential heart and power of our stories. We return to our text and craft it to deepen its focus and power.

Yet sometimes we can cut too much and lose the heart and power of the story. We may impose structure too early. We edit too quickly. We censor, criticize, and condemn before the words are out. It's important to allow ourselves to write our ways to the heart of our pieces, the cen-

---

*Rabbinical literature that explicates and illuminates verses from the Torah, adding extra-textual commentary and stories.

tral metaphors and images that appear as we free our imaginations. At the same time, it's necessary to delete and cut to advance your narrative: As writer Bill Kittredge reportedly stated: "Readers do not want to put their foot on the same step twice."

Gevurah is also the ability to focus on a smaller slice of narrative. In her book *Bird by Bird,* about the art of writing, Anne Lamott suggests cutting out a one-inch window in a piece of paper so that the writer can practice looking at something very closely, magnifying it. Less can be more.

Boundaries and limits shape texts so that they are penetrable, accessible. Think of cutting back the bushes in your front yard so that the path to the front door is clear. You can't let weeds overwhelm the flowers. Yet, an essay also needs weeds, lavish overgrowth, vegetation that just sprouts—writing that appears almost magically from the subconscious. As anthropologist Mary Douglas writes about a garden (from *Purity and Danger*): "If all of the weeds are removed, the garden is impoverished."

On the other hand, some weeding leads to greater growth. The right amount of trimming allows us to tame chaos and create a sense of order, coherence, and beauty.

In this chapter, we'll look at how boundaries and limits are essential to both narrative and sentence structure. We'll also discuss the need to devote ourselves to our work, to take our writing lives seriously.

Focusing on Narrative Structure

Every plot structure requires shaping our text in order to achieve a narrative design. While these designs are more commonly associated with fiction, studying different narrative structures can help essayists think about the most effective ways to order and arrange events in our writing.

The most obvious narrative structure is chronological. It's the way we live, after all. But that doesn't mean that you always have to start in the beginning and close at the end. Memoir and story are not autobiography. In other words, you don't just record what happened to you, day after day, year after year. (Although writer Joe Gould did just that.) As Sven Birkerts remarks in *The Art of Time in Memoir,* there is no better way to smother a memoir than to rely on chronology:

> The point is story, not chronology, and in memoir the story all but requires the dramatic ordering that hindsight affords. The question is not what happened when, but what for the writer, was the path of realization, and it is the highlighting of this that overturns the tyranny of the linear and allows the subtle or obvious implementation of the after the fact perspective.

"The tyranny of the linear." What a beautiful phrase. Writing allows us to escape the oppression of chronology. When you ask somebody how his day was and he answers by recounting the events hour by hour, it can be trying (unless it's your teenage son, in which case you're thrilled that he's speaking to you!). Birkerts says, "Memoir begins not with event but with the intuition of meaning—with the mysterious fact that life can sometimes step free from the chaos of contingency and become story." Instead of viewing life as a chronological series of chance events, the memoirist seeks the pattern of story.

Thus, text is often liberated from the constraints of chronology. As French-Swiss director and screenwriter Jean-Luc Godard says: "There is a beginning, middle, and end . . . but not in that order." For example, Harold Pinter employs reverse chronology in his play "The Betrayal." The first scene takes place after the events of betrayal. The play then moves backward in time, toward the beginning of the characters' indiscretions.

One plot structure mimics the movement of the letter *e.* A story jumps into action, often beginning from the middle of the story (not the end as in Pinter's play). Next the writer circles back to give us background and then jumps forward, continuing on from where the author started toward the ultimate resolution. For example, John McPhee explains in an article for the *New Yorker* that he wrote "Travels in Georgia" in the shape of an *e*. "The story would work best, I thought, if I started not on Day 1 but with a later scene involving a policeman and a snapping turtle. So the piece flashed back to its beginnings and then ran forward and eventually past the turtle and on through the remaining occurrences."

Similarly, in *Bird by Bird,* Anne Lamott states that one can think of plot as A, B, D, C, E. In this model, A is action, B is background, D is development, C is climax, and E is ending.

Again, we begin in the middle of an experience or action without understanding how the characters came to be there. Then the writer fills in the necessary background. By starting in the middle of the story when things are happening, the author hooks the reader, keeping her interested and perhaps a little puzzled. Once the reader is involved in the action, she is more likely to have the patience to plod through the back story, which may be less compelling. Next, the characters and theme are fleshed out and developed. Tension builds until a climax, often one main dramatic event, which brings us to a resolution or ending.

You may choose to delete the first paragraph or the first chapter or chapters of your writing to find the more exciting, potent action. Our first paragraphs are sometimes a kind of throat clearing needed to find the energy of the narrative.

More on the Narrative Arc

Some say there are only two main plot lines: a mysterious stranger arrives in town or a person leaves home—an arrival or a departure. Yet these are really the same because both entail giving up the familiar. Both can be seen as quests that usually employ a narrative arc, a rising motion with tension along the way that is ultimately released: the stranger finds herself accepted in the new town or feels alienated and leaves. A narrative arc typically refers to fiction, but it's also useful to consider when writing memoir. To create an arc for memoir, think of maintaining tension by opposing desire with obstacles. Each time the narrator (or protagonist in a story) satisfies a desire, another obstacle is introduced that keeps the motion of the story rising. You can think of the development as opposing positive and negative charges: as in an atom, the tension bonds the elements together.

As one thread of the story advances, a competing need demands attention. Just when the narrator has almost accomplished his desire, something comes to interrupt its fulfillment. Finally, when the narrator figures out how to overcome the last obstacle, there is a moment of resolution. In essay writing the resolution may be the narrator's hard-won insight.

Some magicians also perform their art by utilizing an arc, which, of course, has a different meaning on the stage. Magician and professional pickpocket entertainer Apollo Robbins says: "The eye will follow an object moving in an arc without looking back to its point of origin, but when an object is moving in a straight line, the eye tends to return to the point of origin, the viewer's attention snapping back as if it were a rubber band" (Adam Green, "A Pickpocket's Tale"). In other words, if there are no hills and valleys, if everything is flat, you will lose your audience's attention. There has to be change. When the narrator faces a series of compelling obstacles, the reader stays engaged: there is tension, narrative momentum—and, maybe, even magic.

It's also possible to think of story as a series of problems and even failures. Writer Benjamin Percy says that we can direct our stories toward a worst-case scenario: the thing we most fear. He calls this the rock-bottom moment, the dark night of the soul, when your character is ready to give up. He offers the example of a couple who long for a child, finally adopt a nine-year-old boy, and then find he was abused and undernourished and behaves like a nightmare. How the parents cope with this painful relationship is the central arc of the story.

Even a simple arc can maintain an audience's interest. A few years ago, when I was speaking about one of my books in Melbourne,

Australia, my husband and I viewed a video in the Melbourne Metropolitan Museum of Art with only one real character, a watermelon, but plenty of drama. Two hands on both sides of the watermelon kept adding rubber bands around its circumference. Only two people's hands were shown. Slowly the watermelon began to take on an hourglass form. The video was surprisingly compelling because there was tension: When would the watermelon finally burst open? Many people gathered watching the video for over a half hour until the watermelon exploded with ripe pink chunks and juice over the floor. It seemed like a surprise even though we all know what's inside a watermelon. Yet the video prodded us to look at a watermelon as if we had never seen one before.

Writer Sven Birkerts offers another model for narrative structure—problem, escalation, eruption, and consequence. In the watermelon video there was a literal eruption. As Birkerts says, in discussing drama, "the main tensions have been discharged and the reader feels that a passage has been fully undergone." The reader feels that she has completed a journey.

Different Essay Structures
The Flash Nonfiction Essay

The flash essay may have a traditional narrative structure, but what distinguishes it is its length—usually under 750 words—and its urgency and energy. The flash relies on concision and compression; it's tightly focused. Because it's so short, you don't have much time to introduce yourself or your topic; it's more like a quick run than a leisurely walk. Writer Dinty Moore says that the flash essay begins in heat, "some burning urgency" ("Field Guide to Writing Flash Nonfiction"). Barrie Jean Borich says that the narrator is searching for the "flash," a decisive moment, a place where the essay rises from narrative into something surprising like an image. You can also experiment with a more associative narrative structure. In addition, the flash is an excellent place to work with material that you had to delete from previous work.

Structures without Narrative Arcs

There are a variety of structures that don't rely on a plot but still have their own logic, their own limits and boundaries.

Episodic Structure

Rather than a traditional plot structure, the author can narrate vignettes with less attention to chronological order. In *Safekeeping* Abigail Thomas says this about the story of her husband's death: "It came in bits and pieces and it needed to be in bits and pieces. My life has no narrative flow, no arc, my remembered life seemed to consist of moments big and small, and it's in these moments that I began to find some truths."

This structure is liberating because there is no need to stick to chronology or to provide transitions. The structure may proceed like an out of order slide show, but if each image is compelling, the reader will stick with you. A central motif and repeating characters create coherence.

The Lyric Essay

The lyric essay is even more fragmented than an episodic structure and reads more like a poem. Logical connections are left to the reader. Often there is no resolution. A lyric essay may be composed of scraps of memory or experience or research or lists or recipes or directions and include multiple voices and points of view. "As a work gets more auto-biographical, more intimate, more confessional, more embarrassing, it breaks into fragments. Our lives aren't prepackaged along narrative lines and, therefore, by its very nature, reality-based art—underprocessed, underproduced—splinters and explodes" (David Shields, *Reality Hunger: A Manifesto*). Thus, the lyric essay may have no final point or theme, other than the way the shards and fragments cohere or contradict each other. Yet it can also be playful, inviting the reader to speculate, reading into the gaps. You may want to separate the sections with spaces and asterisks.

The Braided Essay

The braided essay, a form of lyric essay, weaves two or three elements together, so that the strands join and repeat and part and intersect again, like a braid or a strand of DNA. Brenda Miller's braided essay, "A Braided Heart: Shaping the Lyric Essay," has three main strands: a definition of lyric and braided essays, a narrative about the process of braiding challah, and a story about French braids, as well as some looser wisps about art and massage. There is a pleasing sense of repetition and departure.

The Collage

The collage structure may feel liberating because you don't have to worry how the parts of your writing are going to fit together. You can write a memoir in small manageable chapters, and then piece them together like a crazy quilt. This structure is useful when you really don't know what it is you want to say, and you don't know what your central motif is. The fragments of your experience become pieces that can then be arranged to find pattern. Juxtaposition, the relationships between the pieces, help you clarify meaning. Titles and subtitles also provide coherence. For example, the title "My Children Explain the Big Issues" allows the reader to piece together the vignettes in Will Baker's essay, which otherwise would seem like disconnected random thinking. Without the title the reader would struggle to understand the connection between sections.

Other Structures

Contrast

Developing an essay can be compared to interior design—which sometimes uses a focal point, repetition, and contrast in a room. To create a pleasing design, a center is needed to draw the eye, which establishes a motif (a color or shape) that is then repeated. But there also needs to be opposition, contrast.

Think of constructing an essay based on a contrast—the difference between living in two cities or the contrast between illness and health, for example. In the essay "Joy," Zadie Smith builds her essay by distinguishing joy from pleasure. She tells the reader that she prefers pleasure: she takes indiscriminate pleasure in food, feels pleasure in looking at other people's faces, and then startles us with her insight about joy, the way it colludes with terror because the things that bring us the most joy are also those that can be lost to us—our friends, our children, our spouses.

The Swerve

You can also make a sharp turn in your essays to inject humor, absurdity, or opposition. Find an image or anecdote that's in contrast to the mood you've been developing. If you're writing about something difficult, you can lighten it by including unexpected moments of joy or pleasure. Lee Martin and Sue Silverman call this "letting the light in."

Your essay can also bounce between two topics. For example, I'm writing a memoir now about becoming Israeli, and in between the chapters of my metamorphosis, I give recipes that break up the narrative. You can also insert lists or menus or an email to create a more playful tone, as well as a more interesting and complex rhythm and tempo.

WRITING EXERCISE: A SWERVE

Start by writing about something interesting that happened to you today, and then make a list of what you didn't accomplish or what you ate for lunch, or what you looked at online—to break up the narrative. Be playful. Consider how the list can enhance the meaning of the essay.

Images

As we saw earlier, images can also provide structure for an essay. The last essay that psychiatrist Dr. Oliver Sacks published was called "Filter Fish," a story about gefilte fish, how his mother made it for him as a young child with its viscous gel, and then how, as an adult, he asked his non-Jewish housekeeper to make it for him. When he was dying, he ordered the gentle-tasting gefilte fish from Zabar's. He wrote that gefilte fish would usher him out of life as it had ushered him in. Gefilte fish improbably provides a frame for his life.

Julie Taymor, the movie and theater director, says that she uses a central image to organize all of her productions. In *The Lion King,* for example, she employed "the circle of life" as an ongoing theme. Primo Levi, an Italian chemist who was imprisoned in Auschwitz-Birkenau, wrote *The Periodic Table* and chose chemical elements as the focus of stories. For example, vanadium, a chemical used in making paint, is the title of a chapter about an unexpected epistolary exchange where Levi slowly understands that the man he is corresponding with is, in fact, the Nazi who oversaw him while Levi was imprisoned, a chemist in a German war factory during the Holocaust.

M. F. K. Fisher structured her book according to the alphabet (*An Alphabet for Gourmets*). Anne Morrow Lindbergh structured *Gift from the Sea* according to the shapes and thematic associations of different shells. There's a book whose chapters are based on different sewing techniques, and one structured according to the names of the twenty-six Bikram yoga poses. Judy Gold, a comedian who wrote *My Life as a Sit-Com,* an Off-Broadway show, tells her story onstage through revisiting sit-coms, both those she watched as a child and those she later, as an adult, created and pitched to TV executives.

In all of these the writer is bound by structure, which entails boundaries, gevurah. But these unusual structures also are a form of chesed, kindness, because they give us something to push against, and free us to to be more imaginative, playful, and original.

—

WRITING EXERCISES: DIFFERENT STRUCTURES

- Take an essay you've already written and change the structure. For example, if it's a narrative, try to start at a different place in the story and work backward until you arrive at the original opening. Continue from there.

- Nora and Delia Ephron explored their lives through the outfits they wore in the play *Life, Loss, and What I Wore* (adapted from a book by Ilene Beckerman). Write an essay about three outfits, or three meals, or three songs. Let each item suggest a story and see how they work together and complement each other. You can include a song, an outfit, and a meal in each section.

- Write a story where you invent a structure, one developed according to your own original design. One of my students used the different cars she has driven during her life as an organizing principle, beginning with a VW van in the 1960s.

- Write an essay where you talk about yourself through different parts of the body. (See Phillip Lopate's essay "Portrait of My Body" with its marvelous opening line: "I am a man who tilts.")

- Write a flash essay with discards from previous work.

—✦—

Language

Gevurah teaches us to pare each sentence down to its essentials so the language is most powerful, without excess verbiage. As writers we ask ourselves: Is this word necessary? Is it the right word? The best word? Do we create a rhythm in our prose? On the other hand, do we allow expansive digression when it's interesting and alive?

Also there are tips to make sentences more beautiful. Use muscular verbs and get rid of the verb *to be*. The punch or emphasis of the sentence should come at the end where the sentence culminates. Rid yourself of the passive tense, except where it's needed. Think about letting your main character act, not merely be acted upon.

Use adjectives sparingly or in an interesting way. For example, here is Nora Ephron in "Serial Monogamy": "It [*The Gourmet Cookbook*] had been assembled by the editors of *Gourmet* and was punctuated by the splendid, reverent, slightly lugubrious photographs of food that the magazine was famous for." Notice how the adjective *lugubrious* surprises us and also adds an edge, in contrast with the positive adjectives that come before it.

Furthermore, your sentences should not be monotonous. (The word *monotonous* is monotonous, isn't it? A form of onomatopoeia.) Don't make your sentences all the same length either. There now. Better. My sentences aren't all the same length, are they? Use short sentences to create emphasis. Today.

Sometimes—when it feels right—interrupt your sentences. Don't pare everything down. The rising points of the action, the most interesting and important parts of your story or commentaries, should be emphasized and well developed, fleshed out with enough language to call attention to them.

Finding Time to Write

It's not easy to apply limits and boundaries to our lives. To say no to social obligations, to consecrate time to our writing practice. But the spirit of gevurah teaches us to be resolute. If we want to write, we create a structure, a discipline, to dedicate our time, focus, and energy toward writing.

Yet there is a danger in gevurah—relying too much on structure, discipline, and limits. We also need to invite play and spontaneity and fun into our work—and into our lives. Julia Cameron advises us to have a playdate each week to bring more creativity into our lives, to nourish our spirit and intellect. And sometimes it's more important to have fun than to stick to your schedule. I will usually give up my writing time to play with my grandchildren.

Fear and Awe

The inner emotion associated with gevurah is fear. We fear that our writing is not powerful enough, that nobody will listen to us or care.

That we are wasting our time. We fear that we are not living up to our own or other's expectations. We fear what others will say about us.

Give yourself permission to feel whatever it is you feel. It's OK to be afraid of writing, of exposing your interior life and sharing your truth. You're not alone. Why do you think people spend so much time photographing their meals on Instagram? We're much less vulnerable sharing a meal than we are sharing our souls.

We're all afraid of something. Just make sure to write about it.

WRITING EXERCISE: LIMITS AND FEARS

- Write about saying no, about limits. When were you able to say no and feel good about it? Do you feel guilty about saying no? What role does discipline play in your life?
- Write about a time when you were afraid, mortally afraid. Tell us how you coped or didn't cope. Scream to the world your anxiety and your fear.
- Write about an enemy that you fear. Who or what in your life do you struggle with?

6

HARMONY

Tiferet

TIFERET IS THE COMBINATION OF GEVURAH AND CHESED, kindness and boundaries: harmony. Rabbi Aryeh Kaplan tells us that tiferet is associated with the third day when God separated the sea and the dry land: "The third day set boundaries: not all sea, not all dry land, but a balance between the two." Tiferet, located in the heart, is the sefira of balance and harmony.

Rabbi Elie Munk, a Torah scholar and businessman born in Paris in 1900, describes harmony as life's most basic goal. He states that perfection is static because if a person were to reach perfection, there would be nothing else to attain. Harmony, on the other hand, is ongoing. "It is our purpose to harmonize the threads of being: talents, thoughts, actions, and emotions, so that a person will be in harmony with God's creation."

Harmony doesn't mean that we are in stasis. Rather it's a temporary hard-earned balance. It's telling that Jacob, the biblical figure associated with harmony, struggled with adversity all of his life. He fought with his brother Esav over his birthright, fled his home, was denied Rachel, the woman he wanted to marry, and tricked into marrying her sister, Leah. When he was old and longed for peace and quiet and harmony, his favorite son Yosef disappeared. His other sons had sold Yosef into slavery.

Thus, tiferet, harmony, is not a stopping point but rather an ongoing recalibration of the balance between kindness and limits, abundance and boundaries.

ᵕ· ·ᵔ

An old joke: A Buddhist asked a hotdog vendor for a hotdog. "Make me one with everything." We rarely feel one with everything. Writing stems from disharmony and the desire to redress it. For example, the bestselling book *The Immortal Life of Henrietta Lacks* by Rebecca Skloot is the story of Henrietta's family's need to correct an injustice from the past to establish a new sense of balance and harmony in their lives. When Henrietta was hospitalized with cancer in the 1940s, cancer cells from her body were extracted and cultured to be used for research without permission or profit for the family. (Cancer cells keep growing.) While the family still experiences a strong sense of violation, some family members do come to realize that though they will never own their mother's cells, those cells have benefited the world.

In this chapter we'll examine some facets of harmony—the need, sometimes, for disharmony or discordance; harmony with our audience; metaphor as a type of harmony; and the music of language.

ᵕ· ·ᵔ

A few months ago my husband and I drove to a conference where I would be speaking about my book *The Road to Resilience: From Chaos to Celebration*. On the way to Eilat, my husband missed a stop sign and was pulled over for a ticket, even though he had slowed down and yielded. I was furious with the cops because they were parked there waiting for people to miss the stop sign, which was very hard to see and was at the end of a road with a high speed limit. The odds were stacked against anyone actually seeing that sign.

We got out of the car, and I felt even more angry because we were paying a lot of money to attend the conference and I didn't want to add a huge fine to that sum. I tried to talk my way out of a ticket. I have to admit that I did not feel very resilient when the policeman wouldn't listen to me. Then the police stopped another car behind us, filled with a group of religious men all dressed in black coats and hats. They were Breslovers, followers of Rebbe Nachman who lived in the late eighteenth century in Ukraine. They all got out of the car, and one immediately began to twirl around, dancing and singing a tune, a *nigun*. I asked one of them: "How can you be so happy? You're going to get a big ticket." He answered: "You'll see when you get up to heaven. This money, you don't have to worry about. It's *tzedekah* [charity] for the state of Israel. You don't have to be upset about it."

I laughed. Sometimes life and writing offer the opportunity for reframing experience or, in more academic terms, cognitive restructuring, a paradigm shift—finding a moment of harmony and balance where none seems to exist.

~ · · ~

Language can also be thought of in terms of harmony and balance. In telling our stories we struggle to find the appropriate language, words that are in harmony with the experience we are describing. Yet sometimes it makes more sense to shun that harmony. Aharon Appelfeld, an only child from Bukovina, lived a charmed life with his well-to-do parents before the Second World War. But his innocent life was shattered when he was in grade school: his mother was murdered by soldiers and he was imprisoned in a concentration camp in Transnistria. A young boy, he fled from there alone and survived in the forests and by living with peasants. Here's what he has to say about words (from *The Story of a Life*):

> I've carried with me my mistrust of words from those years. A fluent stream of words awakens suspicion within me. I prefer stuttering, for in stuttering I hear the friction and the disquiet, the effort to purge impurities from the words, the desire to offer something from inside you. Smooth, fluent sentences leave me with a feeling of uncleanness, of order that hides emptiness.

Stuttering, in this case, is more appropriate than fluency. Sometimes the more easily that language comes to us, the more it covers up our vulnerability. When my Hebrew was much weaker, I worked in the hospital on the cancer ward as a pastoral counselor, and some of my most profound experiences occurred because I couldn't speak fluently. I was there to listen and to be a humble presence. I couldn't resort to any usual response. Nor did I offer any words about my own situation. My silence allowed me to "read" and focus on the patient.

Truth

Tiferet also means *truth*. It's interesting, though, that the biblical character Jacob, known as the man of truth, was both deceitful and also the victim of deceit. Jacob lied to his father, Issac, to attain the birthright that was supposed to be his brother Esav's. Later Jacob's father-in-law, Laban, lied to Jacob, giving him Leah for his wife instead of his love, Rachel. Truth seems like it should be simple, yet it seldom is.

Before creating Adam, God said, "Let us make man" in the plural. The commentary in the Midrash tells us that God consulted with the angels. The angels were divided into different groups. Love said, "Let him be created, and he will do loving deeds." But Truth said, "Let him not be created because he will be all deceit." Righteousness said, "Let him be created because he will do righteous deeds." Peace said, "Let him not be created because he will be all quarrelsome and discord."

What did God do? He seized hold of Truth, and "he cast truth to the ground" (Daniel 8:12). "Then the angels said to God, 'Why do you despise your Angel of Truth? Let Truth rise out of the earth, as it is said, 'Truth springs out of the earth'" (Genesis Rabbah 8:5).

This story demonstrates that our ability to know the truth is limited and partial. Each of us holds a fragment of fractured truth. That is why it is so important that we tell and share our stories because only then can a larger truth be illuminated.

Thus, every narrative is a portion of the truth. Ask siblings the story of their childhood, and everyone has different parents. Similarly, when you tell a story, it's from your own angle (I almost wrote *angel*—interesting) of perspective. Certain details have to be omitted to emphasize the thrust or theme of the story. The writer is like a pilot who has to make sure that the narrative as craft is launched and carried on the path it establishes for itself so that it lands in one piece. Otherwise, the craft may not lift off the ground or it may be bound for nowhere. To do so, the writer has to heighten certain aspects of the story and diminish others.

WRITING EXERCISE: ONE TRUE THING

My teacher, novelist William Giraldi, asked his students to write one true sentence about their fathers. That one true sentence can form the kernel of an essay.

Harmony and Enlargement

Harmony can also be thought of as the writer's ability to situate the story in terms of a larger context, to connect with a wider world. The self swings between the narrow confines of the personal life and the greater spaciousness and expansiveness of the world at large.

For example, you may choose to let the news of the day or the landscape outside your home reverberate with the more personal text of your story. A few years ago in Israel, there was an emergency preparedness exercise in case of an earthquake. Everybody was supposed to receive a message on their cell phone at 11 a.m. telling them to go outside to practice for an emergency. (I'm still not sure what that entailed.) This event was juxtaposed with the fact that my daughter had left for her first day of college. Though my daughter's departure was not an emergency, the separation was also a small—maybe not so small—earthquake in my life for which I was not entirely prepared. The juxtaposition provided an echo of similarity: the external world offered a psychological symbol for an internal emotional state.

In this excerpt from the novel *The Last of Her Kind* by Sigrid Nunez, the narrator situates the characters in a very particular context: the historical moment shapes the characters' attitudes, fate, and destiny:

> It was the year of Tet, the year of the highest number of casualties in Vietnam. It was the year of the Prague Spring, the year of the assassinations of Robert Kennedy and Dr. King, the year the Democratic National Convention turned bloody (it was also the year of My Lai, but we were not yet aware of it).

James Baldwin begins his essay "Notes of a Native Son" by situating his family story in the drama of a larger historical moment:

> On the twenty-ninth of July , in 1943, my father died. On the same day, a few hours later, his last child was born. Over a month before this, while all our energies were concentrated in waiting for these events, there had been, in Detroit, one of the bloodiest race riots of the century. A few hours after my father's funeral, while he lay in state in the undertaker's chapel, a race riot broke out in Harlem. On the morning of the third of August, we drove my father to the graveyard through a wilderness of smashed plate glass.

Baldwin later interprets the political violence that accompanies the death of his father as a personal message, viewing the events as "a corrective for the pride of his eldest son. I had declined to believe in that apocalypse which had been central to my father's vision; very well, life seemed to be saying, here is something that will certainly pass for an apocalypse until the real thing comes along."

The personal and the political are interwoven and dramatically resonate.

A more lighthearted example: In "Serial Monogomy" Nora Ephron comments on her personal experience by juxtaposing seemingly unrelated events: "Just before I moved to New York, two historic events had occurred: the birth-control pill was invented and the first Julia Child cookbook was published." Notice how those events coalesce in her next sentence: "As a result, everyone was having sex, and when the sex was over you cooked something."

Writing Exercise: Your Personal History

Research what happened on the day or month or year that you were born. Begin an essay with that information and then explore how that event has paralleled or contrasted with your own personal history in some way.

Metaphor and Simile as Harmony

Metaphor and simile are ways of connecting two seemingly disconnected things and revealing a surprising harmony. Simile uses *like* or *as:* My love is like a red, red rose. Metaphor leaves out the connecting *like* or *as* and makes a direct link: All the world's a stage. Two disparate objects have something startling in common and can be understood in terms of one another.

Poet Mark Doty calls metaphor "an unexpected collision." James Dickey goes even further:

> The deliberate conjunction of disparate items which we call metaphor is not so much a way of understanding the world but a perpetually exciting way of recreating it from its own parts, as though God—who admittedly did it right the first time—had by no means exhausted the possibilities. It is a way of causing the items of the real world to act upon each other, to recombine, to suffer and learn from the mysterious value systems, or value-making systems, of the individual, both in his socially conditioned and in his inmost, wild, and

untutored mind. It is a way of putting the world together according to rules which one never fully understands, but which are as powerfully compelling as anything in the whole human makeup.

A way of creating and reinventing the world, recognizing oneness where it doesn't seem to exist. Things that seem disparate have something in common, a unity. For example, in *The City in the Sea,* Edgar Allan Poe compares a sea to a wilderness of glass.

In *Paris to the Moon,* Adam Gopnik creates a more prosaic simile, the similarities between French bureaucracy and an exercise machine.

Every French ministry is like a Nautilus machine, thoughtfully designed to provide maximum possible resistance to your efforts, only to give way just at the moment of total mental failure. Parisians emerge from the government buildings on the Isle de la Cite feeling just the way New Yorkers do after a good workout: aching and exhausted but on top of the world.

Paris sounds a lot like Israel.

Victor Lodato begins his story "Jack, July" with this powerful metaphor: "The sun was a wolf. The fanged light had been trailing him for hours, tricky with clouds." Lodato's crisp metaphor—the sun as a wolf—is original and stunning.

Here are two examples of similes that express surprising connections:

- "My return to Naples was like having a defective umbrella that suddenly closes over your head in a gust of wind." (Elena Ferrante, *The Story of a New Name,* Neapolitan Quartet)
- "The interesting ones are like islands," he said. "You don't bump into them on the street or at a party. You have to know where they are and then go to them by arrangement." (Rachel Cusk, *Outline*)

Writer Bret Anthony Johnston suggests formulating similes and metaphors by combining different senses: sight, vision, hearing, touch, or taste. This technique is called *synesthesia,* a merging of senses where, for example, somebody visualizes colors when they hear music. Hearing and vision became one. Another example: when the Jewish people were given the Torah at Mount Sinai, they saw the voice of God.

When constructing metaphors and similes, we can merge two or more senses to make interesting comparisons. Johnson gives an example of this synthesis of senses from Amy Bloom's story "Silver Water":

> My sister's voice was like mountain water in a silver pitcher, the clear
> blue beauty of it cools you and lifts you up beyond your heat, beyond
> your body.

Instead of making a comparison that links two auditory images, Bloom links sound (her sister's voice) with vision (water in a silver pitcher) and touch (cools you).

In her poem "The Fish," Elizabeth Bishop describes the fish's bulk not only in terms of weight but also of sound:

> *He hung a grunting weight*

Here's my own example, which links the auditory and the visual:

> When the congregation murmured the final prayer of Yom Kippur,
> Neila, it was as if a flock of storks suddenly lifted off from dark
> concrete, whirled into the air, and flew off, flapping their enormous
> wings, forming a point or, more accurately, a mathematical symbol,
> the one that means greater than or less than, depending on your
> point of view.

WRITING EXERCISE: MAKING METAPHORS AND SIMILES

Write a metaphor or simile by merging two senses. Complete these sentences:

> The sound of the children's laughter on the swings [was like/was] . . .
>
> The smell of the stew on the stove [was like/was] . . .
>
> The singing on Friday night [was like/was] . . .
>
> Reading a bedtime story to my children [is like/is] . . .
>
> The knife was as sharp as . . .
>
> The mountains were lit by an orange light as if . . .

Dialogue as a Mode of Discord

Of course, drama requires conflict. Sometimes, though, conflict is not stated directly, only alluded to. Whole stories are written with the real subject in subtext because what needs to be expressed is too dangerous to voice out loud. Talking about the taboo subject will upset the status quo that has been created, the apparent harmony. Think of how many families avoid certain subjects—secrets, hurtful topics, the names of dead loved ones, anything that causes pain or longing.

"Hills Like White Elephants," Hemingway's story of a couple discussing an abortion, is told almost all in dialogue: the man and woman have a conversation at a café in a train station without mentioning the problem they're struggling with. The emotions are understated, written in code. The abortion is the elephant in the room—the unstated issue that looms over everything, like the hills in the distance.

Dialogue, of course, is often used to describe overt conflict as well as to reveal character. Consider this passage from *Jazz* by Toni Morrison:

> "I need my breath now." Violet tests the hot comb. It scorches a long brown finger on the newspaper.

"Did he move out? Is he with her?"

"No. We still together. She's dead."

"Dead? Then what's the matter with you?"

"He thinks about her all the time. Nothing on his mind but her. Won't work. Can't sleep. Grieves all day, all night . . ."

"Oh," says the woman. . . . "You in trouble," she says, yawning.

"Deep deep trouble. Can't rival the dead for love. Lose every time."

That beautiful passage portrays the discord and conflict in the relationship, how the dead can be perfect, while the living are so flawed.

Dialogue can also reveal the hurtful way that people don't listen to one another, even when one is speaking about something close to his heart. In Chekhov's short story "The Lady with the Dog," the protagonist, Dmitri Gurov, tells his fellow card player about his deep fascination with the woman he met in Yalta. The acquaintance replies, "You were right this evening: the sturgeon was a bit too strong!" Not everyone can be a good listener, but when we are talking about something close to our hearts and the listener doesn't listen at all, it can feel particularly painful.

Though we don't always use dialogue in essays and memoir, it's useful to think of the narrator of your essays as being in dialogue with the self, layers of persona in conflict with one another, parts of the self in conversation, competing voices that create disharmony or static. The narrator may then choose to reconcile those voices, to find a point of temporary harmony or stasis. Or not.

―――

Writing Exercise: Talking to Yourself

Write a story where you talk to yourself about a problem you are going through. Let layers of your personality be in conflict with one another.

It's really not that bad. It could be a lot worse. I mean who cares how I look? I'm still a good person, a caring person, a loving aunt. A person is what she is on the inside, right? But my thighs rub when I walk.

I want another piece of red velvet cake, the one my mother used to bake before. Before all that bad stuff. I am going to bake that cake. But I shouldn't. Maybe I will just go check if I have the recipe. I know that there's baking soda and vanilla extract in the house 'cause I made those chocolate chip cookies. No, no, I can't stop thinking about how much weight I've gained in the past four months. I gained eighteen pounds in four months. I don't know what I was thinking. My mom told me why they called it red velvet. Like that dress she bought me. I don't know how I got fat. Or maybe I do.

―

Music

Writers learn to be sensitive to the music of language, attuned to the harmony of its sound and meaning and nuances. Writers read their work aloud so that they can hear when a word is out of tune, when the rhythm is off, when the meaning isn't quite right.

Here's writer Leonard Michaels on the music of writing (from "My Yiddish"):

> Ultimately, I believe, meaning has less to do with language than with music, a sensuous flow that becomes language only by default, so to speak, and by degrees. In great fiction and poetry, meaning is obviously close to music. Writing about a story by Gogol, Nabokov says it goes la, la, do, la la la etc. The story's meaning is radically musical. I've often had to rewrite a paragraph because the sound was wrong. When at last it seemed right, I discovered—incredibly—the sense was right. Sense follows song.

Read your work aloud to yourself or to somebody else. Then you can hear when something doesn't work.

In an interview in the *New Yorker,* "Long Story Short" by Dana Goodyear, Lydia Davis, the acclaimed writer of very short stories, explains how when she writes or reads, she pays attention to an inner sense of language.

> "I've gotten very alert not just to mixed metaphor but to any writing mistake," she said. "A little bell goes off in my head first. *I know something's wrong here.* Then secondly I see what it is." She opened the notebook and read a sentence about an acute intimacy that had eroded into something dull. "Acute is sharp, and then eroded is an earth metaphor," she said. She read another: "'A paper bag stuffed with empty wine bottles.' I thought about that. You'd think he could get away with it, but he can't, because 'stuffed' is a verb that comes from material. It's soft, so it's a problem to stuff it with something hard."

A sensitivity to both sound and meaning may be what distinguishes good writers. They're attuned to the nuances of language. This sensitivity isn't just about being accurate; it's also sourced in a love of words.

WRITING EXERCISE: DISCORD AND MUSIC

- Write a dialogue where two people are in conflict. Each has a desire that is at odds with the other's. As the dialogue progresses, put more obstacles in their way. Raise the stakes. As you come to the end of the dialogue, see what happens. Have the characters reached some kind of resolution or are they even more polarized?
- Write a dialogue where it's clear that the two people are not listening to each other.
- Every story can be thought of as a war. Write an essay about a fight that you had with somebody. Plunge the reader into the chaos and discord.
- Read one of your essays aloud to somebody. Now let somebody read it to you. Listen to its music.

Thinking about Audience

Harmony also means that we are concerned with our audience. If you say something that everybody has heard before, you bore your audience and lose your reader. You are not in harmony with your audience's intellect and needs.

When you write, you might imagine talking to a specific person so that you can choose what you say and how you say it—your tone and diction. That will help you determine how intimate you want to be with your reader, the language you'll choose. Pretend you're writing to a friend or an aunt or a professor. What will keep them reading? What do you know that they don't? Make sure your first sentence and paragraph draw them in.

Also feel free to turn to the audience at times and engage with the reader directly, using the second person. You involve the reader more closely when you ask him or her a question. Here's an example from a student essay: What should I do? I wondered. What would you do?

WRITING EXERCISE: MY DEAR FAMILY

Write a letter to a family member who you never met. Tell him or her about your life. Include a family story and a family saying. See what happens.

Beauty

Tiferet also suggests beauty. Today I saw a bright-green lizard on the bark of a eucalyptus tree and watched as his eyes turned to look at me, little brown beads that revolved in their sockets, 360 degrees. He grasped the tree with the pads of his extended claws and extended his back legs. "Beautiful sounds, sights and smells revive a person," says the Talmud.

There is a beauty of symmetry and harmony, but there is also a beauty of imperfection. In Japanese gardens, for example, a path may contain an irregular number of stones. This sense of being off balance replicates the beauty of nature where nothing is perfect. Not everything has to match. In ceramics the technique called *wabi sabi* allows for the beauty of irregularity. A bowl is not perfectly oval; a patina is irregular. It may be the writer's job to convey unexpected beauty to the reader, like the beauty in the wear and tear of aging.

The worn, scratched wooden night table next to my bed was passed down to us by my husband's great-aunt. It used to bother me that it was chipped and scratched, and I thought that I should paint it or sand it, yet never got around to it (It's a little embarrassing to admit, but I don't know how to do it). One night, my husband and I went out to dinner near Ashkelon in a restaurant where we sat at a scratched wooden table. As I looked around, I noticed that all of the tables were scratched, beat-up wood. In fact, the surfaces looked a lot like my night table. The owner of the restaurant told me that the tables were scratched on purpose, in fact it was a style—distressed. Now I respect my table for revealing something of its life, having a history. I am able to see its (distressed) beauty.

A Lack of Certainty

The challenge of the sefira of harmony is to allow discord and chaos. If the writer tries to present an experience as if there are no hesitations, questions, or problems, then the writing may not engage the reader. When everything is presented as flawless, there is no story and no possibility of achieving insight. Think of it this way: a pearl is created from the dirt that gets into the oyster's shell. There needs to be friction for something interesting, unlikely, and beautiful to emerge. Don't be afraid to admit your uncertainty. Tell people about the discord, chaos, and trauma in your life.

WRITING EXERCISE: WITHOUT RESOLUTION

Write about something that is troubling you as if you were talking to a loving friend or a therapist. Don't try to solve anything. Just let the story speak for itself. If something embarrasses you, note that but keep writing.

ENDURANCE
Netzach

NETZACH (ENDURANCE OR ETERNITY), which is on the same line as kindness (the right side of the body), allows us to move through the world with determination. Its inner quality is confidence, the audacity to take a stand, express an opinion, believe in oneself. It allows us to overcome the obstacles that prevent us from asserting ourselves.

Netzach comes paired with the quality of *hod,* the sefira that means surrender. These two sefirot are compared to the legs of the body: netzach the right leg, hod the left.

Netzach is associated with the fourth day of creation: the stars and sun and moon were created on that day, fixed forever in their orbits. Netzach, steadfast and enduring, has a sense of assurance, a stubbornness. It's forthright, ready to argue and stake a claim, but it doesn't have to yell. To express our voice in the world, to write and continue writing, to endure in our writing, we need netzach.

In this chapter we'll look at the quality of endurance: the need to state a bold opinion, accept and learn from the criticism of fellow writers, weather rejections from publishers, and persist in our work.

◡ · ‿ ◡

After I had two books published and had won a National Jewish Book Award, I expected that the publishing gates would open. I was wrong. Not only did I have to struggle to get published, I was also humiliated in a fiction writing group.

The first time I attended that group, I was anxious because I only knew one member of the group and I had just started writing short stories. I had no idea how the others would receive me. At the meeting there were two of us who were new. Mona was much younger than me, but she seemed like a good writer. During the evening somebody gave writing prompts, lines from a poem that we used as starting points for stories. Then somebody presented a short story she had been working on. I didn't say much. I didn't feel that it was my job to pronounce judgments at the first meeting. Besides, I try to be a gentle critic, believing that change and growth come when a person feels supported, not when they feel attacked.

I still remember the first comment that my poetry teacher gave me in 1978, when I was twenty-two and just starting my master's degree in creative writing at Colorado State University. I read the poem I had handed out to the other eight students in the writing group, and this is what my professor said: "This sounds like the poem of a fifteen-year-old girl." He didn't say it as a compliment. I was devastated.

I was totally taken aback when before the next meeting of the fiction writing group in Jerusalem, I mistakenly received a group email sent from one of the participants. The message went something like this: "Maybe Sherri knows how to write, but I don't think she knows anything about how to critique. She didn't seem very bright. Mona, the other new person, was fantastic, really sharp. I don't know. Maybe if we coach Sherri, give her some books on writing fiction, she'll catch on— but I'm not so sure that she is right for the group."

You have to understand that I was teaching creative writing at the time.

My mother used to say *a good life is the best revenge*. But now I see, writing well may really be the best revenge.

I decided to stay in the group. I have some of the qualities associated with netzach like persistence and stubbornness and the ability to endure rejection. (Not that I like it. It still hurts. Oh boy, does it hurt!) The next meeting I submitted a story, and the participants gave me a few helpful comments. But the woman who had written the evil email asked me: "Are you sure that you understand the concept of the short story? That the character has to act, not just be acted upon?" And she later said: "Some of this dialogue is just deadly."

I felt humiliated, but again I told myself that I had received a National Jewish Book Award and that this woman had probably never had anything published.

A few days later I sent the story off to a short story contest in *Moment* magazine judged by Erica Jong. Six months later the magazine called, and I thought that they wanted to sell me a subscription. Instead, I learned that I had won first prize, publication, a thousand dollars, and a trip to LA for the awards ceremony.

Endurance, persistence, fortitude. A kind of faith. Because there are so many people who will put you down and humiliate you, tell you that you don't know much, that you can't do this and not to waste your time.

Who are they to speak? And who are you not to?

ᴗ · · ᴗ

Moses, the biblical figure associated with netzach, learned about endurance as he led the Hebrew people through the wilderness. At first, when God spoke to him and told him that he would bring the Israelites out of Egypt, he questioned God's command. He didn't feel like he was the right person to lead the nation. It was difficult for him to speak. He stuttered. "Who am I that I should go to Pharaoh and bring the Israelites out of Egypt? . . . Who am I to lead the people to Israel out of Egypt?"

God showed him the burning bush, a symbol of endurance. Even when it seemed that the bush should have burned up and been destroyed, it continued to blaze—a message to Moses that what seemed most difficult would not annihilate him. Eventually, he found his voice and became the greatest leader of the Jewish people. A man who stuttered became a man who was able to lead the people through forty years in the desert. He was able to fight for the people when they disbelieved, when they lost their faith.

I am the codirector of the Koby Mandell Foundation, which runs programs and camps in Israel for bereaved children and families. In partnership with comedian Avi Liberman, we run comedy fundraisers twice a year with stand-up comedians who have been featured on American late-night television shows and on Netflix specials. My husband and I introduce the show, and we always tell a joke. Last year I told a terrible joke. In fact, I forgot the joke in the middle. Later, I talked with one of the comedians about how to tell a joke. He told me: "You have to walk in, plant the microphone, and own the stage."

We are so hesitant in our lives to own the stage, but netzach tells us that there are times when we need to be sure, certain, confident, ready to fight for our beliefs, ready to make a claim, even when others may not agree with us.

The danger of netzach is that you become too much of a bulldozer and alienate others because you don't listen to them. You may get too involved in polemics or dogma. Netzach comes paired with hod so that we don't become obstinate but remain supple and pliable, no matter how great our passion.

Devotion

In *Outliers* Malcolm Gladwell describes research about becoming great: to excel at something, you have to devote at least ten thousand hours of work. That means sitting at your desk and writing, thinking, reading, revising. At first, writing's a tough discipline, and then it may turn into a pleasurable need (at least sometimes). The brain has a plasticity: the act of writing paves new neural pathways. Once those pathways are formed, traversing those pathways allows you to enter a concentrated state of focus. To be in the flow. Sometimes.

As a writer you need endurance and persistence, the ability to continue even when it seems that nobody could give a raisin about your work. When my children were young and napping, I wrote children's stories, and I kept sending them out and guess what? The editor of a prestigious publishing house called me and told me that she was interested in publishing the picture book. A few weeks later, I got a letter that they had decided not to take it. But I kept writing. Thirty years later, I had my first picture book published, *The Elephant in the Sukkah*. After I broke my ankle, when I entered the *sukkah*, the temporary hut that some Jewish people construct for the holiday of Sukkot, I felt like an elephant with my walker, like there was no room for me. And the story was born. I hope it doesn't take you thirty years to achieve your writing dreams, but sometimes it does take a lot of time. (Of course, that's not true for everybody.) And today you can publish your own work more easily or post it on Facebook or Instagram.

Writing can be seen as an act of devotion, a calling. You have to keep working, often alone. You may have to tell yourself that your writing has value no matter what the outside world tells you. You have to believe in yourself even if nobody else does.

Virginia Woolf says this about the need to persevere (from *A Writer's Diary*):

The creative power, which bubbles so pleasantly in beginning a new book, quiets down after a time, and one goes on more steadily. Doubts creep in. And then one becomes resigned. Determination not to give in, and the sense of an impending shape, keep one at it more than anything.

Netzach allows us to keep steady, determined, and patient, waiting for the shape of our work to be revealed, while hoping to one day find an audience for our work. My agent, Anna Olswanger, is now shopping around another children's book that I wrote, and she told me that perseverance and patience are the keys to getting a book published: netzach and hod.

Finding a Focus

We don't just endure or persevere. Netzach teaches us to focus, even with the terrible distraction of all of our electronic devices. When we aren't working or taking care of a family and we do have time to write, we turn away from our email, Kindle, or apps and narrow our attention to concentrate on our writing. To create a diamond, carbon has to be stressed under enormous pressure, under high temperatures, deep in the earth for billions of years—yes, billions!

In addition, netzach enables us to focus our story through a particular lens. For example, in the Neapolitan Quartet, a four-novel series, Elena Ferrante concentrates on the relationship between two friends from childhood, and that compression magnifies the complex emotional bonds of their relationship.

The Structure of an Argument

Netzach also teaches us to think about writing as an act of persuasion. We have an argument, a claim that we want to make. We want others to understand our thinking, our opinions. We can think of structuring arguments through asking four main questions: What is it? Why is it? How is it? And what should be done be done about it?

The first question: What is it? allows us to describe the particulars of a phenomenon that interests us. The next question: Why is it? analyzes how something came into being, its history. Then we evaluate the subject's worth—why it's good or bad—or which parts are positive, which are negative—and finally we make a proposal—what should be done about this issue? This four-part structure allows us to think logically through an argument. In addition, we have to anticipate the reader's objections to our argument and refute those claims.

Of course, when we write essays and memoirs, we're not usually writing straight-up arguments, and especially not proposals, but this structure may be useful to you in organizing your thoughts or straightening out a first draft.

Netzach as A More Expansive View

Netzach also means eternity, which is of course, timeless, something that endures, one of the attributes of God. By using the lens of netzach, we can extend our stories, relating to what happened before we came on the stage, before the start of our own personal stories. The present can be infused with the past.

WRITING EXERCISE: WHAT CAME BEFORE

Write about where you live and what happened in your town before you arrived there. You can describe the town's history or geography or geology. Use the word "before" at least three times.

WRITING EXERCISE: PERSIST AND INSIST

- Netzach is also related to *nitzachon,* the Hebrew word for "victory." Success is often a matter of persistence, endurance, refusing to give up. Write about what success means to you and a time you were successful.
- Write about a time in your life when you were persistent, even stubborn, when you refused to give in.
- Write a letter of complaint to a person, place, or company you are displeased with. Be firm, courteous, and creative. Lydia Davis wrote a very short story called "Letter to a Funeral Parlour" that was a letter of complaint to a funeral director who had called her father's remains *cremains,* a word that she felt showed disrespect and insensitivity.
- Write a letter of complaint to a part of your body.

8

SURRENDER

Hod

WHILE NETZACH IS THE POWER OF ENDURANCE, *hod* is the ability
to surrender. Hod was created on the fifth day, the day that the first
living creatures, fish and birds, were created. Both fish and birds move
about more freely than other animals—fluidly, easily, and gracefully.
They aren't bound to the gravity of this world.

While netzach is unchanging, hod is malleable, flexible, supple,
humble. But surrender is not a synonym for defeat. Instead, there's a
glory associated with surrender, a beauty. Aaron, Moses's older brother,
is the biblical figure associated with hod. While Moses was fiery and
unyielding, Aaron was more flexible, known as a man of peace. If cou-
ples did not get along, he was able to help them bridge their differences.
A midrash tells us that thousands of babies were named after Aaron
because he brought people together in peace. When his two children
were killed after bringing a strange fire into the temple, we are told that
Aaron was silent. He was able to contain himself even when suffering,
even when the ways of God did not make sense. (Or maybe he was simply stunned into silence by the trauma.)

In this chapter we'll look at surrender in terms of a narrator's
humility and empathy. We'll also explore some additional meanings of
hod: to admit, thank, and praise.

Humility

Hod is on the left side of the body, the same side as gevurah, the ability to restrain oneself. Sometimes, even in a very personal essay, the primacy of the *I* can be minimized, as the narrator turns her focus to others or other subjects. For example, in "Six Glimpses of the Past: On Photography and Memory," Janet Malcolm begins her essay, which is structured by photographs, by describing a famous painting:

> I am looking at two pictures. One is a color reproduction of Ingres's great 1832 portrait of Louis-François Bertin, a powerfully bulky man in his sixties, dressed in black, who sits with both hands assertively planted on his thighs, and engages the viewer with a look of determination touched with irony. The other is a black and white snapshot of a two or three-year-old girl taken by an anonymous photographer sometime in the nineteen thirties. The young child has assumed Bertin's pose.

In a later paragraph she tells us: "The young child in the snapshot is me."

Even though the essay details Malcolm's family history, the narrator portrays herself as curious instead of narcissistic or self-involved. She offers the reader entrance to a world larger than just her particular family.

Yehuda Amichai's poem "Tourists" also delays the introduction of the *I*. It begins:

> *Visits of condolence is all we get from them*
> *They squat at the Holocaust Memorial.*

It's not until the second stanza that the poet turns to the *I*.

> *Once I sat on the steps by a gate at David's Tower, I placed my*
> *two heavy baskets at my side. A group of tourists was standing*

around their guide and I became their target marker. "You
see that man with the baskets? Just right of his head there's an
arch from the Roman period. Just right of his head." "But he's
moving, he's moving!"

I said to myself: redemption will come only if their guide tells
them, "You see that arch from the Roman period? It's not
important: but next to it, left and down a bit, there sits a man
who's bought fruit and vegetables for his family."

The reader identifies with the humility of the narrator, while the poem
is actually an assertion of the primacy of the personal, eclipsing the historical. Amichai tells us that the man who has been shopping deserves
more attention than the ruins.

WRITING EXERCISE: EKPHRASIS—ART AS LITERARY DEVICE

Write about a work of art that you connect to. Start by describing a painting or sculpture and then tell the reader how you respond to that work of
art, what it means to you. Highlight the art and artist, but also convey how
your own thoughts or story connect with the painting or sculpture.

Point of View

The flexibility of hod offers empathy, allows us to imagine and acknowl-
edge other points of view. "When I write a story I am all the characters
in it," says Israeli fiction writer Etgar Keret in an interview about his
story "Creative Writing." Even when writing a memoir, you can open
yourself to other points of view. For example, as the narrator you can
use phrases like this: "I imagine what my mother was thinking that
day." "I believe my husband saw that . . ."

The stork is called *hasidah* in Hebrew, which means "the devout or the loving one" because storks give so much love to their mates and their young. Yet the stork is classified in the Bible as a nonkosher bird. Why? Because storks give love only to their own. In other words, the stork does not extend its empathy. Hod, on the other hand, allows us to expand our compassion.

WRITING EXERCISE: WRITING FROM DIFFERENT POINTS OF VIEW

Childhood Incident

- Write a story about a childhood incident but write it in third person. As Abigail Thomas says in *Safekeeping: Some True Stories from a Life*: "There are things you can say in the third that would sound maudlin in the first."
- Write about a difficult choice you made, one that you may feel guilty about. Now write the same story in the third person. Does that narrative distance change the story in any way?

A Family Photo

Pick a family photograph or a photograph that has meaning for you. Describe the picture in the third person as if you were a stranger looking at it. Don't write now about any personal meaning it holds for you. What is the quality of the photograph? Grainy? Dark? Torn? What is the lighting like? What is the time period when the photo was taken? What is in the background? What do the participants look like? What are they wearing? What are they holding? What is the expression on their faces? What has happened to bring them together?

Now, on another sheet of paper, pick one of the people in the photograph and imagining that you are that person, write an intimate monologue of your thoughts and feelings. I wrote about a photograph of my grandmother working behind the counter in her Brooklyn lingerie store in the 1920s and imagined her displeasure when a customer wanted to bargain down the price.

Next write about the photo as if you were the photographer. What is going through your head as you take the picture? What is your relationship to the subjects and how do you feel about them?

In the first or second person, write to one of the people in the photograph from their future. What do you want to tell them that they don't yet know?

Finally, write about what happened before and after the photo was taken.

Put these sections together, omitting what doesn't seem important, developing what interests you the most. Leave white space between the sections, especially when there are changes in point of view.

You can also exchange photos with another writer and imagine the story of the photograph without knowing anything about it.

⟿

Unusual Points of View

We may surprise ourselves and our readers as we perceive the world from a unique perspective. For example, in Margaret Atwood's story "Stone Mattress," at one point the narrator reflects from the point of view of a raven. Verna, now an older woman, debates murdering a man she has met on a cruise to Alaska, as she slowly realizes that he is the boy who raped her when they were in high school, the person who ruined her life. Pregnant, she was sent to a home for unwed mothers and had to give away the baby.

> A raven flies overhead, circles around. Can it tell? It is waiting. She looks down through its eyes, sees an old woman—because, face it, she is an old woman now—on the verge of murdering an even older man because of an anger already facing into the distance of used-up time. It's paltry. It's vicious. It's normal. It's what happens in life.

Somehow by writing from the raven's point of view, the narrator normalizes her desire for murder.

Atwood's poem "A Drone Scans the Wreckage" also takes an unusual perspective, that of an inanimate object of war, to shock us out of our complacency.

Point of view is not only a matter of perspective or empathy but also of power. The person who tells the story most often owns the story. In his book *The Art of Perspective: Who Tells the Story,* Christopher Castellani argues that the narrator of the story is the person who is empowered to tell the story. But he is also the person who bears responsibility for it.

WRITING EXERCISE: EXPANDING OUR PERSPECTIVE

- Describe a landscape as seen by a bird. Do not mention the bird.*
- Write an essay about a disturbing incident that you experienced. Now rewrite the essay from the point of view of someone else who was involved. How does the new perspective change the story?
- Write a story about a time you were lost. Now tell the story from the point of view of an animal or object that witnessed you.
- Write an essay about any topic in the second person (you). The following excerpt is from "Second Person," an essay by Ehud Havatzelet.

You've sworn never to write a piece in Second Person.

You ask yourself why. Lorrie Moore and Jay McInerney did it well. Eudora Welty has that great story, right? Someone once told you there was a whole French novel written in Second Person.

You remember you don't read French.

You've heard Second Person is inclusive, it brings the reader into the fray, a character's divorce or the search for lost car keys or rollicking good sex becomes yours. Second Person establishes a dialogue with the reader, you've been told, unlike First Person, a neurotic's whining, or Omniscience, a dialogue with God, who doesn't even have the manners to answer back.

---

*From *The Art of Fiction* by John Gardner.

Surrendering to the Material

Writer Joan Leggant describes the text a writer accumulates as inventory, available to be worked with. The famous maxim of Chekhov is similar: if in the beginning of the book, there's a rifle hanging on the wall, by the end of the work the gun should be fired. Use what you have. Richard Powers describes the process of the first draft as a writer scattering crumbs, suggesting a path for the writer to return to in further drafts. The writing tells you where you need to go.

The process of writing also requires surrender, submitting to the unconscious. In addition, sometimes you have to take a break from the work to allow the ideas to percolate so that you can receive what you need to continue writing. In the *haftorah** for Chanukah we read Zecharia's prophecy: *not by might or power, but by my spirit.*

Get up from your writing. Do the dishes or cook and eat dinner. Go for a walk. Your subconscious is still at work. Silas House, a novelist, playwright, and nonfiction writer says (from "The Art of Being Still"):

> The No. 1 question I get at readings is: "How many hours a day do you write?" I used to stumble on this question. I don't write every day, but when I first started going on book tours I was afraid I'd be revealed as a true fraud if I admitted that. Sometimes I write for 20 minutes. Other times I don't stop writing for six hours, falling over at the end like an emotional, wrung-out mess, simultaneously exhausted and exhilarated. Sometimes I go months without putting a word on the page.
>
> One night, however, I was asked that question and the right answer just popped out, unknown to me before it found solidity on the air: "I write every waking minute," I said. I meant, of course, that I am always writing in my head.

Voices

Sometimes, when we write, it may feel as if we are talking in voices, as though God is speaking through us. The voice of the piece comes to us,

---

*Selections from the books of Nevi'im (Prophets) that are publicly read in synagogue on Shabbat and holy days after the Torah portion.

alive and vital. The writing takes off by itself. I'm sure you have read about the author who says that his characters take over the story, and he sits back and listens to them. Poet William Blake said that while writing some of his poems, he felt he was taking dictation.

The writing arrives as a gift. Yet the danger in the sefira of hod is the writer who believes that his work should always be an inspired meeting with the muse. In my experience, it's our job to create a home for that inspiration when it's willing to visit us. Hod comes paired with netzach, endurance and persistence, so that while we wait for inspiration, we keep slogging on.

Gratitude

Hod is also related to *hoda-ah,* the Hebrew word for "praise"—the ability to appreciate the beauty and glory of the world, to feel and express gratitude. Although many essays are written about discomfort and anxiety, we can write essays about experiences that lead us toward appreciation. What or who do you appreciate? Who do you honor? What experiences are delightful, even blissful? James Wright's poem "A Blessing" describes an exalted encounter with horses on the side of the road. Here's an excerpt:

> *They ripple tensely, they can hardly contain their happiness*
> *That we have come.*
> *They bow shyly as wet swans. They love each other.*

We can also be grateful for those writers whose work is most important to us. Which writers do you appreciate? Whose work do you love reading?

Admitting Our Mistakes

Hod also means "to admit": to admit weakness or vulnerability or uncertainty. We can continually reevaluate our claims, opinions, and feelings. We can admit that we are ambivalent about an experience or decision. We can admit to lying. For example, in Brenda Miller's essay "The Date," she tells us that she is willing to let her date view the unvarnished person on her refrigerator door, the notes and pictures underneath magnets there. But later on in the essay she says, "I lied. I changed everything on my refrigerator, on my bulletin board, on my mantelpiece."

We can give ourselves permission to be wrong as in this excerpt from the poem "Winter Stars" by Larry Levis:

> *I got it all wrong.*
> *I wound up believing in words the way a scientist*
> *Believes in carbon, after death.*
>
> *Tonight, I'm talking to you, father, although*
> *It is quiet here in the Midwest, where a small wind,*
> *The size of a wrist, wakes the cold again—*
> *Which may be all that's left of you & me.*
>
> *When I left home at seventeen, I left for good.*
>
> *That pale haze of stars goes on & on,*
> *Like laughter that has found a final, silent shape*
> *On a black sky. It means everything*
> *It cannot say. Look, it's empty out there, & cold.*
> *Cold enough to reconcile*
> *Even a father, even a son.*

The poet doesn't just admit a mistake. He takes responsibility and allows for the possibility of reconciliation.

WRITING EXERCISE: FAILURES AND MISTAKES

- Write an essay about a mistake that you made.
- Write an essay about a scar, wound, illness, or accident.

- Write about a great failure, a stupendous failure, when you or someone you love made a total mess of things.
- Write an essay about something you were once certain about and now need to reevaluate. You can start "Once I knew . . ."

⟶

Patience

Hod relates to a deep patience with one's work. We return to the writing over and over, paying attention to what is present and what is missing. We may have to wait, to be silent, to pay attention, to trust that more will be revealed. Patience is a form of humility, an ability to dwell in uncertainty. It tells us that even though we are working toward a finished text, we cannot hurry the process.

⟶

WRITING EXERCISE: BE PATIENT, PLEASE

- In an interview in *Makor Rishon,* an Israeli newspaper, Israeli screenwriter and director Rama Burshtein says that waiting and prayer are essential elements of her creative process. As you write, talk to God about the process. Wait and see where you are guided.
- Write an essay about patience. When are you patient? What are you most impatient about? How do you cope with impatience?
- Write an essay that is a meditation on an object or a pastime, on prayer, aging, weddings, or funerals. Let your mind enter the topic as fully as you can. Linger. Be curious. Slow down. You can address the reader if you want, using words like *behold* or *look.*

⟶

9

CREATIVITY
Yesod

YESOD IS THE JUNCTION OF *NETZACH* AND *HOD*. Paralleling the sixth day of creation, the day that human beings were created, yesod is the sefira associated with sexuality and creativity. God created us to create—babies, ideas, machines, technology, stories.

Jewish thought tells us that each day brings a new creative energy to the world, a rejuvenation. We have the possibility of re-creating ourselves, seeing things anew, writing texts that lead us toward a deeper, more profound bond with the world. Acting in the world as God's creative partner.

In the Torah after God promises Moses that he will lead the people out of slavery, when Moses asks God his name he answers: *I will be what I will be.* God, who is perfect in every way, encompasses an aspect of becoming. We, too, are in the act of becoming, and our creativity offers us the possibility of reinvention and transformation.

Yet every act of creativity involves a descent into chaos and darkness. "The kernel which is sown in the earth must disintegrate so that the ear of grain may sprout from its pieces. Strength cannot be resurrected until it has dwelt in secrecy. Putting off a shape, putting on a shape—these are done in the instant of pure nothingness" (Martin Buber, *Ten Rungs: Collected Hasidic Sayings*).

Some people find it hard to create something new because they resist chaos and uncertainty and reach conclusions too quickly, seeking control. They rush toward what they already know. But every act of true creativity demands that we dwell in mystery.

Yosef, the biblical character associated with yesod, found redemption and renewal after he had dwelled in the dark space of prison, where he correctly interpreted the dreams of another inmate, Pharaoh's former butler. Pharoah was the ruler of Egypt, and when, years later, he too had a perplexing dream, Yosef was summoned to solve it. Yosef then became Pharaoh's chief adviser, implementing a plan to rescue the Egyptian people from seven years of famine. Rabbi Aryeh Kaplan tells us that Pharaoh gave Yosef a new name, Zaphnath-Paaneah, which means "revealer of secrets." Creativity involves a similar process—the ability to dwell in and unravel mysteries. In this chapter we'll look at different means of generating and enhancing creativity.

Creativity as Invitation

The Chassidic masters tell us that everything that happens to us is a lesson. But it is also an invitation to create:

One summer, I was driving behind a trailer truck that was transporting giant blocks of limestone on its long narrow bed. The blocks looked like enormous tombs. The truck inched forward slowly because of the weight of its load, and it was impossible for me to pass it on the curvy road.

That image stayed in my mind, and it wasn't until I sat down to write that it became a symbol of grief in my story "Jerusalem Stone," which is about a woman who is threatened by the heavy weight of the grief she carries as a young widow, struggling to create a new life for herself and her son.

Later that week I read a newspaper article about physicists who were conducting experiments to create new chemical elements, exploding electrons to create new atoms. I realized that my character would be a physicist—even though I have never studied physics. The next day, I picked up a woman hitchhiker from my community who, it turned out, was getting a PhD in physics. I asked her how scientists went about creating a new element, and then I wrote the story. A little scientific knowledge can go a long way in writing fiction. I invented a narrator who was trying to explode atoms in order to create a new element. That scientific goal became a metaphor for the narrator who also wanted to reinvent herself. I wove disparate events in my life together to form a narrative that had its own logic and emotional momentum.

WRITING EXERCISES: CREATIVE PLAY

Different Domains

Combine two or three seed ideas that are not necessarily connected and create friction.* See what emerges. Creativity often arises when you bring different domains together, people or objects or categories that are not generally associated with each other, for example, as I do in this book—Kabbalah and essay and memoir writing.

For example, write three hundred words about bathing suits and then write three hundred words about cake. Now write a third short essay that brings these two topics together in some way.

Enhancing Creativity

Stuart Schoffman, the late journalist who wrote a weekly column for a Jerusalem magazine for many years, told me that he made sure that he was constantly learning, that it was key to maintaining a long creative life. Learn something new today.

One way to stimulate creativity is to invoke the other side of your brain. Try writing with your nondominant hand for a few minutes. Doing this can help you bypass the rational brain, which wants to write about what it already knows.

---

*Adapted from "Smushing Seed Ideas Together" by David Michael Kaplan in *Now Write! Fiction Writing Exercises.*

- Write about the block you grew up on, the games you played as a child.
- Write about money. A time you lost money. Found money. Worried about money. What money means in your life. Use the phrases: "Once I thought" . . . . as well as "But it is also true" in the text.
- Write about noises. What noises soothe you? What noises bother you?
- Write an essay that includes three different colors.
- Write about a gift you received. Or write about a gift you would like to receive or give.
- Ross Gay wrote an essay, "Tomato on Board" about carrying a tomato plant through an airport. Write about something you carried—for example, a musical instrument, a suitcase, or a cake.
- Write about an object that you lost.

Cutting In

When I was a graduate student, I attended a workshop with Robert Bly who offered this exercise:

Pick a fruit or vegetable. Describe it in detail. Now look at it and describe it again, this time comparing it to a parent or child or friend. How is it similar? Dissimilar? Next cut the fruit or vegetable open. Describe your relationship with the person you chose by writing about what you see inside. What do you discover?

Prompts

Writing prompts are phrases and sentences that stimulate you to write. You can incorporate them into your text: in the beginning to get you started or in the middle to keep you going or at the end to find a way of closing. Or in all of those places. Pick one of these and begin:

His feet pounded the pavement.

It wasn't real.

What wouldn't you do?

Five minutes ago, they'd had so much to say.

There wasn't a moment that she didn't have the same thought.

Aging isn't a horse race.
The man looked like somebody she used to know.
Her son slammed the door shut.
You could use some lipstick.
It wasn't my favorite holiday.

I was in a workshop with Linda Stern Zisquit, a Jerusalem poet, who asked us to write ten words or phrases about faith. Then she asked us to write ten words that pertained to hope. We used these phrases to kick-start poems or essays.

Aphorisms

When I was in college my professor, Albert Goldbarth, assigned this exercise for writing a poem, but it also works for essays.

Think of an *aphorism,* which the dictionary defines as "a terse saying embodying a general truth": for example, *you can't have your cake and eat it too.* Now create your own aphorism, but by the end of the poem or essay, reverse the aphorism.

I still remember what I wrote forty years ago. I started with this aphorism: *dancing is taking off from the beat* and arrived later at *dancing is landing on the beat.*

Clustering

Clustering is a technique of doodling where you visually brainstorm the associations that flow from an idea. Begin with a word (for example, *hair*) and write it in the middle of your page, drawing a circle around it. Then free associate by writing other words and experiences that you associate with the word *hair,* drawing circles around those words and phrases. Draw lines between the circles and scribble connecting phrases and sentences there.

When you are ready to write, pick some of those words and phrases and see how they fit together and keep you writing (adapted from an exercise by Gabriele Rico in *Writing the Natural Way*).

Implementing

The sefira of yesod is also the ability to implement. Yosef wasn't just a dreamer: he also organized the Egyptian people and economy to weather a seven-year famine, storing food so that everybody would be able to eat.

We need to send our work out into the world, to find our audience. You may start a blog or join a writers' group or send your work to friends before posting it online or in newspapers and journals.

Don't think you have to publish right away in the most prestigious national literary journals. Think local. Years ago, I had an essay published in the *Washington Post* but was having problems finding publishers for my other work. I spoke to an acquaintance, Tovi Glasner, who was a puppeteer, and she told me: *write for the Jewish world.* I immigrated to Israel soon after, and before I left, I spoke to Eric Rozenman, then the editor of the *Washington Jewish Week,* who offered me a column, writing about our first year in Israel. What was amazing: I discovered even hard, trying experiences could be used for material. It was much easier to wait in the Interior Ministry for hours when I knew I could use the experience as a columnist—and be paid for it!

Find an outlet for your work. Post or submit something today.

10

RULERSHIP
Malchut

MALCHUT MEANS KINGSHIP, which we can think of as authority or rulership. This sefira is associated with voice, your unique take on the world: your language, tone, enthusiasm, patience, maturity, humility, humor, crankiness, and passion.

Malchut is the sefira connected to King David, who was a poet. Malchut is usually depicted as residing at the feet, but it is also sometimes described as centered in the mouth, the voice. King David gave voice in the Psalms to his difficult and dramatic life: He fell in love with Bathsheva, a married woman, and sent her husband off to battle to die. Bathsheva gave birth to his son, but the baby died. King David's son Amnon, by his second wife, Ahinoam, raped his half-sister, Tamar, David's daughter. Avshalom, another son, killed Amnon in vengeance and tried to steal King David's leadership. It's not surprising that the Book of Psalms contains a full range of feelings: poems of deep despair as well as immense gratitude.

As the last sefira, malchut receives from and is derived from all of the other sefirot. You have learned to engage keter, your will and desire to write. You have found inspiration (chochmah) and developed your writing in a comprehensive way (bina). You've written from the fullness of your heart and have found the heart of your essays (chesed). You've learned to create boundaries (gevurah), editing based on the theme and purpose of your writing. You've emerged from conflict to find points of insight and harmony (tiferet). You've persisted (netzach), believing in your projects, and at the same time, you've surrendered (hod) to allow the writing to speak to you. You know the difference between forcing the text and waiting for its spirit to reveal itself. You've found sources of creativity (yesod).

Now is the time to take command of your kingdom. The word *author* is connected to the word *authority:* a call toward mastery, command of our imaginative powers, judgment, and creativity.

In this chapter we'll first look at topics that we have "mastered," as well as the way writing allows us to master time. And then we'll turn to the variety of voices available to us.

Becoming an Expert

We all have subjects in which we are experts. My students are artists, dancers, writers, teachers, and former high school principals; all have written beautiful work on these subjects. Because I live in Israel, I have an authority to write about life in Israel, about being an immigrant. I can also write about Torah and religious subjects and yoga. I am also an expert in grief and mourning—and resilience.

Once I asked a group of adult students: "What are you experts in?" They had a hard time answering because they didn't think of themselves as authorities. But when I said, "I am an expert in being messy," one said that she was a master in procrastination, another a master in suffering. One said that she was very good in surrendering her own needs even when she shouldn't. Those were all topics that they didn't at first consider worthy.

Write a list of ten topics that you feel that you are an expert in or would like to be an expert in.

Playing with Time

Malchut allows us to transcend time because we can master time in our narratives: we enter the present, the past, and the future at will. We can speed time up or slow it down. We can focus deeply on a few minutes or an hour. We can write about two days ten years apart as Virginia Woolf does in *To the Lighthouse*. A minute can take ten pages. Ten years can go by in one sentence.

For example, Joyce Carol Oates begins her novel *The Gravedigger's Daughter* with a thirty-page description of a girl's half-hour walk next to the Erie Canal. The girl worries that she's being stalked by a man in a panama hat, that she's in danger of being raped or killed. The reader experiences the girl's anguish, anxiety, and terror as time slows down and almost stops.

Ian McEwan slows down time to describe the terrifying split-second moments of a car accident in *The Child in Time:*

> He was preparing to overtake when something happened—he did not quite see what—in the region of the lorry's wheels, a hiatus, a cloud of dust, and then something black and long snaked through a hundred feet towards him. It slapped the windscreen, clung there a moment and was whisked away before he had time to understand what it was. And then—or did this happen in the same moment?— the rear of the lorry made a complicated set of movements, a bouncing and swaying, and slewed in a wide spray of sparks, bright even in sunshine. Something curved and metallic flew off to one side. So far Stephen had had time to move his foot toward the brake, time to notice a padlock swinging on a loose flange and "wash me please" scrawled in grime. There was a whinnying of scraped metal and new sparks, dense enough to form a white flame which seemed to propel the rear of the lorry into the air.

Writing can also slow down time for events that we celebrate. You can write about your child's first birthday party, remembering the way that you gave each child a white belt made of crepe paper and taught the children karate in the backyard. The almond trees were just beginning to blossom. When you imagine the richness of the moment, the smells and tastes and texture of the air, what you and others were saying and doing, you enlarge the moment to emphasize it. Or you may speed up time to summarize five years in a paragraph. In short, writing allows us to transcend time.

Signaling Time Change

Although we can skip around in time, writers should identify when *now* is in the text, a present moment from which the writer is communicating. The reader needs to be situated in both time and place. As long as the writer locates the reader in time, the writer can move backward into flashbacks through the simple use of verb tense or markers like *three weeks before*. The writer can also advance into the future with signals: *She didn't know that three weeks later, the music teacher would ask her to perform in a concert and she would meet her cousin for the first time.* The writer can also signal that more than one event is occurring at the same time by using the word *meanwhile*. This magical word gives the writer the chance to layer the story with concurrent happenings.

WRITING EXERCISE: A MATTER OF TIME

- Slow down time. Write about a short period of time, five minutes of your life. Show us all of the telling details. Take your time. Fill in the picture.
- What is your notion of time? Are you always late? Early? Why? Write about missing something because you couldn't get there on time.
- The first commandment given to the Jewish nation in the Torah is the one to sanctify time by marking the month of Nissan, the month that the Jewish people were liberated from their slavery in Egypt. Pick a time in your life where you felt liberated from some type of

enslavement. It could be an addiction, a bad relationship, a sense of hopelessness, or even boredom. Tell us the story.

- Write an anecdote having to do with work. Then use the word *meanwhile* to tell another story that was happening at the same time.

WRITING EXERCISE: SCENE AND SUMMARY*

Write about a mystifying or painful event that happened in childhood. Write about the next ten years in a summary. Speed time up in this section: "For the next ten years, we would . . ." Now write about the event from the retrospective perspective of an adult. Begin with "What I didn't see or understand then . . ."

---

*Adapted from "Moving through Time" by Nancy Reisman in *Now Write! Fiction Writing Exercises.*

Persona

In Hebrew the word for face, *panim,* is plural. We have many faces. Although we aim for authenticity, when we write an essay or memoir, we may also create a dramatic persona to convey our truths. As Phillip Lopate writes in his piece on writing essays, "On the Necessity of Turning Oneself into a Character":

A good place to start is your quirks. These are the idiosyncrasies, stubborn tics, antisocial mannerisms, and so on that set you apart from the majority. . . . to establish credibility, you would do well to resist coming across as absolutely average. Who wants to read about that bland creature, the regular Joe? The mistake many would-be essayists and memoirists make is to try so hard to be likable and nice, to fit in, that the reader, bored, begins craving stronger stuff (at the very least, a tone of authority). Literature is not a place for conformists and organization men.

One writer describes his voice as the ability to pretend that he is speaking to somebody after his second glass of wine: in other words, his defenses are slowly stripped away and he becomes more authentic. You don't have to stand naked, but you do have to take off your coat.

If you are the mother of young children, let yourself be the mother of young children, the *uber* mother. Tell us about your disappointments and fears and conflicts and victories but make them big.

While some writers have naturally distinctive voices, we can also construct dramatic voices by reading and learning and experiencing, by trusting in our own authority. As Sarah Manguso notes, in her *New York Times* article "Green-Eyed Verbs":

> My least favorite received idea about writing is that one must find one's voice, as if it's there inside you, fully formed and ready to turn on like a player piano. A voice is what emerges from an informed intelligence as it reaches toward accurate perception.

In other words, you don't suddenly discover your voice. You build it over time. You think, read, and write. You study the world and a voice emerges from inside of you. In her article "When You Write a Memoir, Readers Think They Know You Better Than They Do," Dani Shapiro observes:

> I am striving to make order out of chaos, which is the sweetest pleasure I know. When I succeed, I have a thing, this story, to offer. It isn't me. It isn't even a facsimile. I have used my life—rather than my life using me—to make something more beautiful and refined than I could ever be.

After I wrote my memoir, *The Blessing of a Broken Heart,* many people exclaimed that I was so honest in my book. But the book is only a part of my story. I left a lot out of that book, pages where I was crying out in total despair. I didn't tell everything, and the voice I adopted while telling the story is only a part of me—a wiser more patient woman than I was at the time. Still, the narrator I crafted was a help to me because she offered me wisdom in a period of darkness and chaos. I crafted that book, and its order and authority offered me temporary control and solace. In shaping that book, I also shaped myself.

WRITING EXERCISE: PERSONA: WHO IS THE NARRATOR?

In the beginning of her memoir *Wild,* Cheryl Strayed writes:

> I'd been so many things already. A loving wife and an adulteress. A beloved daughter who now spent holidays alone. An ambitious over-achiever and aspiring writer who hopped from one meaningless job to the next while dabbling dangerously with drugs and sleeping with too many men. I was the granddaughter of a Pennsylvania coalminer, the daughter of a steelworker turned salesman. After my parents split up, I lived with my mother, brother, and sister in apartment complexes popu-lated by single mothers and their kids. As a teen, I lived back to the land style in the Minnesota north woods in a house that didn't have an indoor toilet, electricity or running water. In spite of this, I'd become a high school cheerleader and homecoming queen, and then I went off to college and became a left wing feminist campus radical.
>
> But a woman who walks alone in the wilderness for eleven hundred miles. I'd never been anything like that before. I had nothing to lose by giving it a whirl.

Your reader probably doesn't know who you are. Write down at least six things that you want your reader to know about you, for example:

> I am a mother and a bereaved mother. I am a good wife in training. I am a pastoral counselor who is tired of counseling. I like doing headstands, but for short times. I worry that there will be enough food for the holi-days. I have a dog who keeps rising from the dead.

Tone

As writers, we cultivate voices that gush and confess or voices that restrain themselves with dignity or detachment—or travel between both states. We can be cranky, disturbed, and neurotic. We can be funny, silly, forgiving, understanding, and learned. We can be broken, revealing disappointment and rupture. We can be literary. We can be coarse. We can take a measured view like E. B. White, be vulnerable and intimate like Anne Lamott, or be bold and elegant like Joan Didion.

In the essay "Goodbye to Forty-Eighth Street," E. B. White writes as a thoughtful, reasonable gentleman, perplexed by the steadfast weight and power of material objects as well as the sadness in life. He creates a persona the reader feels is trustworthy:

> For some weeks now I have been engaged in dispersing the contents of this apartment, trying to persuade hundreds of inanimate objects to scatter and leave me alone. It is not a simple matter. I am impressed by the reluctance of one's worldly goods to go out again into the world.

His diction is elevated, for example he uses the word *dispersing* instead of *tossing*. His tone is one of genial amusement.

Ross Gay's book *The Book of Delights* is a record of things and events that delight him. In one essay in the book, "Inefficiency," Gay uses parentheses, many clauses, repetition, incomplete sentences, and interruptions like "I should say," to create an engaged . . . vivid persona.

> I don't know if it's the time I've spent in the garden (*spent* an interesting word), which is somehow an exercise in supreme attentiveness—staring into the oregano blooms wending through the lowest branches of the goumi bush and the big vascular leaves of the rhubarb—and also an exercise in supreme inattention, or

distraction, I should say, or fleeting intense attentions, I should say, or intense fleeting attentions . . .

Gay begins with doubt, a statement of uncertainty as he admits that he doesn't know if it's the time in the garden that has made him pay attention, an act of supreme attentiveness, which as he states, is also an exercise in supreme inattention, or intense fleeting attentions. Notice how he qualifies himself as he writes, including the reader in his quest to understand the sublime nature of inefficiency.

Joan Didion's tone in "Why I Write" is unapologetic, bold:

Of course I stole the title for this talk, from George Orwell. One reason I stole it was that I like the sound of the words: Why I Write. There you have three short unambiguous words that share a sound, and the sound they share is this:

I

I

I

In many ways writing is the act of saying I, of imposing oneself upon other people, of saying *listen to me, see it my way, change your mind*. It's an aggressive, even a hostile act. You can disguise its aggressiveness all you want with veils of subordinate clauses and qualifiers and tentative subjunctives . . . but there's no getting around the fact that setting words on paper is the tactic of a secret bully.

In an interview with the *Paris Review,* novelist Elena Ferrante states that she begins with a composed narrator who gradually loses control so that a more agitated voice emerges. She explains:

I only know one thing for certain—it seems to me that I work well when I can start from a flat, dry tone, that of a strong, lucid, educated woman, as many middle-class women are today. At the beginning I need curtness, a terse, clear, unaffected language, without ornamentation. Only when the story begins to emerge safely, thanks to that tone, do I begin to wait for the moment when I'll be able to replace those well-oiled, quiet links with something rustier, raspier, and with a pace that's disjointed and agitated, even at the growing risk of the story falling apart. The moment I change register for the first time is both exciting and anguished. I enjoy breaking through my character's armor of good education and good manners. I enjoy upsetting her self-image, her will, and revealing another, rougher soul underneath, someone raucous, maybe even crude. I work hard to make that change in register come as a surprise and also to make it seem natural when we go back to a more serene style of narration.

We all have civilized and uncivilized voices battling for control inside us. Tone, conveyed by syntax, word choice, pacing, and imagery, is a marker of that tug-of-war inside us, a kind of face-off between the superego and the id. Yet even when the reader feels that the narrator's mask has been removed, and the narrator is no longer trying to save face and is showing herself as raw, real, and authentic, the narrator's persona is still usually crafted and composed.

—

Writing Exercise: Experiment with Voice
Emotional Tone

- Write about a childhood experience. Now write about the same experience from the perspective of a very angry child or as an agitated adult.
- Write a love letter that is sickeningly sentimental.
- Write a hate letter that seeks vengeance.
- Write an essay where you use a phrase that you heard often in your childhood. Repeat that phrase at least three times in the essay.

- Write about a time that you felt powerful. How did you use this power? What happened afterward?
- Are you fed up? Write a rant about something that you can't stand and won't put up with anymore.

Authority

- Write about authority in your life. Write to somebody who had authority in your life. Let that person know the effect he or she had on you.
- Think of what knowledge or skill you are completely confident about. When do you speak with authority? Write about that.

Persona

At a workshop Brandel France de Bravo gave us this exercise:

- Think of a story that has a lot of emotional resonance for you, that is still charged in some way. Now meet with a partner and tell the other person your story. The other person doesn't speak but takes notes. Switch. Then write up your partner's story but narrate it so that you create a persona who is telling the story. Try to pour emotion into the story. Imagine your way into your partner's story. Feel free to add what you need to create a dramatic narrative from what they have shared. Use poetic license. Read the story to your partner.
- In Psalm 118, it says, "Today is the day that God invented. Rejoice and be glad in it. As Ross Gay does, write about something you see today that delights you. Use repetition, interruptions, and interjections to create a breathless, excited, enthusiastic persona.

A FINAL WORD

IN THE TORAH GOD SAID, *LET THERE BE LIGHT,* and there was light, creation. We too create our own worlds with words. We write to illuminate those worlds. *Olam,* the word for "world" in Hebrew, also means "hidden." By engaging with the sefirot, what was hidden in your life may become revealed, manifest.

Nobody else can tell your truth. Rabbi Nachman says: "Each shepherd has his own special song as does each blade of grass."

"Everything in the world can be imitated except truth. For truth that is imitated is no longer truth," says Rev. Menachem Mendel of Kotzk.

Take the words and experiences and knowledge that God has granted you, your truth, and write your memoir. Be bold, creative, patient, free, and focused as you craft your life into art. Your readers are waiting for you.

WRITING EXERCISE: YOUR BOOK LAUNCH

Envision yourself holding a book in your hands as you give a reading. What is the title of the book? As you introduce your work, what will you say to your audience?

BIBLIOGRAPHY

Amichai, Yehuda. "Tourists." In *The Selected Poetry of Yehuda Amichai.* Translated by Stephen Mitchell. Berkeley: University of California Press, 1996.

Appelfeld, Aharon. *The Story of a Life.* New York: Schocken, 2006.

Atwan, Robert. "Foreword: Confessions of an Anthologist." In *The Best American Essays.* Edited by Edwidge Danticat. Boston: Mariner, 2011.

Atwood, Margaret. "A Drone Scans the Wreckage." *New Yorker,* August 13, 2012.

———. "Stone Mattress." *New Yorker,* December 11, 2011.

Baldwin, James. *Notes of a Native Son.* Beacon Press, 1955.

Barrington, Judith. *Writing the Memoir.* Portland, Ore.: Eighth Mountain Press, 1997.

Barry, Lynda. *What It Is.* Montreal, Canada: Drawn and Quarterly, 2008.

Bascom, Tim. "Picturing the Personal Essay: A Visual Guide." *Creative Nonfiction,* no. 49 (Summer 2013).

Baxter, Charles. *The Art of Subtext.* Minneapolis, Minn.: Graywolf Press, 2007.

———. *Burning Down the House.* Minneapolis, Minn.: Graywolf Press, 2008.

Birkerts, Sven. *The Art of Time in Memoir.* Minneapolis, Minn.: Graywolf Press, 2008.

Bishop, Elizabeth. "The Fish." In *Poems.* New York: Farrar, Straus, Giroux, 2011.

Buber, Martin. *Tales of the Hasidim: The Early Masters.* Translated by Olga Marx. New York: Schocken Books, 1975. First published 1947.

———. *Ten Rungs: Collected Hasidic Sayings.* Translated by Olga Marx. London: Routledge, 2002. First published 1947.

Cameron, Julia. *The Artist's Way*. New York: TarcherPerigee Books, 2016.

Carver, Raymond. *Cathedral*. New York: Knopf, 1983.

Castellani, Christopher. *The Art of Perspective*. Minneapolis, Minn.: Graywolf Press, 2008.

Chekhov, Gustav. *The Lady with the Little Dog and Other Stories*. London: Penguin Books, 2020.

Dickey, James. "Metaphor as Pure Adventure." Lecture. Coolidge Auditorium, Library of Congress, Washington, D.C., December 12, 1967. Audio recording, 50 min.

Didion, Joan. *The Year of Magical Thinking*. New York: Random House, 2007.

———. "Why I Write." *New York Times*, December 5, 1976.

Dillard, Anne. "Coming of Age in Pittsburgh: To Fashion a Text." *Wilson Quarterly* 12 (1988).

Doty, Mark. *The Art of Description: World into Word*. Minneapolis, Minn.: Graywolf Press, 2010.

Douglas, Mary. *Purity and Danger: An Analysis of Concepts of Pollution and Taboo*. London: Routledge, 1966.

Earling, Debra Magpie. *Perma Red*. New York. Blue Hen, 2002.

Elbow, Peter. *Writing without Teachers*. New York: Oxford University Press, 1998.

Elliot, T. S. *Four Quartets*. Orlando, Fla.: Harcourt Brace, 1974.

———. "Tradition and the Individual Talent." In *Selected Prose of T. S. Eliot*. Edited by Frank Kermode. London: Faber and Faber, 1975.

Ellis, Sherry, ed. *Now Write! Fiction Exercises from Today's Best Writers and Teachers*. New York: Penguin, 2006.

———. *Now Write! Nonfiction*. New York: Penguin, 2009.

Ephron, Nora. "Serial Monogamy" in *I Feel Bad about My Neck: And Other Thoughts on Being a Woman*. New York: Knopf, 2006.

Ferri, Sandro, and Sandra Ferri. "Elena Ferrante: Art of Fiction No. 288." *Paris Review*, no. 212 (Spring 2015).

Fisher, M. F. K. *An Alphabet for Gourmets*. Berkeley, Calif.: North Point Press, 1989.

Foster, Patricia. "Creating Shape in Scene." In *Now Write! Nonfiction*. Edited by Sherry Ellis. New York: Penguin, 2009.

Franklin, Jon. *Writing for Story*. New York: Plume, 1986.

Fremon, Celeste. "Shrapnel." In *Now Write! Nonfiction*. Edited by Sherry Ellis. New York: Penguin, 2009.

Freud, Sigmund. "Negation." *International Journal of Psycho-Analysis* 6, part 4 (October 1925).

Gardner, John. *The Art of Fiction*. New York: Random House, 1991.

Gay, Ross. *The Book of Delights*. Chapel Hill, N.C.: Alqonquin, 2019.

Gessen, Keith. *A Terrible Country*. New York: Penguin-Putnam, 2019.

Gilbert, Elizabeth. "Thoughts on Writing." Elizabeth Gilbert website.

Goldberg, Natalie. *Writing Down the Bones: Freeing the Writer Within*. Boston: Shambhala, 1986.

Goodyear, Dana. "Long Story Short." *New Yorker,* March, 2014.

Gopnik, Adam. *Paris to the Moon*. New York: Random House, 2001.

Gordon, Emily Fox. "Confessing and Confiding." *American Scholar,* March 4, 2015.

Gordon, Mary. *Circling My Mother*. New York: Anchor Books, 2007.

Green, Adam. "A Pickpocket's Tale." *New Yorker,* January 7, 2013.

Gladwell, Malcolm. *Outliers*. London: Penguin, 2009.

Greer, Andrew Sean. *Less*. Boston: Abacus, 2018.

Haber, Yaacov. *Sefiros*. White Plains, N.Y.: Torah Lab, 2008.

Hall, Donald. *Essays after Eighty*. New York: Houghton Mifflin Harcourt, 2014.

Havatzelet, Ehud. "Second Person." "Opinionator," *New York Times,* July 14, 2014.

Hemley, Robin. "Your First Kitchen." In *Now Write! Nonfiction*. Edited by Sherry Ellis. New York: Penguin, 2009.

Hiestand, Emily. "Hose." In *Short Takes*. Edited by Judith Kitchen. 254–260. New York: W. W. Norton, 2005.

Hill, Kathleen. *She Read to Us in the Late Afternoons: A Life in Novels*. Santa Monica, Calif.: Delphinium Books, 2018.

Hiss, Tony. *The Experience of Travel*. Chicago: Taylor and Francis, 2012.

House, Silas. "The Art of Being Still." "Opinionator," *New York Times,* December 1, 2012.

Hunt, Laird. "A Bottle of Water in Brazzaville." "Opinionator," *New York Times,* July 21, 2013.

Johnson, Bret Anthony. *Naming the World and Other Exercises for the Creative Writer*. New York: Random House, 2008.

Kaplan, Aryeh. *Inner Space: Introduction to Kabbalah, Meditation and Prophecy*. Brooklyn, N.Y.: Moznaim, 1990.

Kaplan, David Michael. "Smushing Seed Ideas Together." In *Now Write! Fiction*

Writing Exercises from Today's Best Writers and Teachers. Edited by Sherry Ellis. New York: Penguin, 2006.

Kephart, Beth. "Required Reading." *Creative Nonfiction,* no. 49 (Summer 2013).

Kincaid, Jamaica. *My Brother.* New York: Noonday Press, 1998.

Kingsolver, Barbara. "A Talk in the Woods." *Poets & Writers,* December 2018.

Kitchen, Judith and Jones, Mary Paumier. *In Short: A Collection of Brief Creative Nonfiction.* New York: Norton, 1996.

Kiteley, Brian. *The 3 A.M. Epiphany: Uncommon Writing Exercises That Transform Your Fiction.* Cincinnati: Writer's Digest Books, 2005.

Koch, Kenneth. *Wishes, Lies and Dreams: Teaching Children to Write Poetry.* New York: Harper Perennial, 1999.

Kois, Dan. "Lynda Barry Will Make You Believe in Yourself." *New York Times Magazine,* October 30, 2011.

Kooser, Ted. "Hands." In *In Short: A Collection of Brief Creative Nonfiction:* Edited by Judith Kitchen and Mary Paumier Jones. New York: Norton, 1996.

Labowitz, Shoni. *Miraculous Living.* New York: Simon and Schuster, 1996.

Lamott, Anne. *Bird by Bird.* New York: Bantam Doubleday Dell, 2016.

Leiner, Yaakov. *Beit Yaakov.*

Leonard, Elmore. *10 Rules of Writing.* New York: HarperCollins, 2007.

Levi, Primo. *The Periodic Table.* New York: Schocken, 1995.

Levine, Sara. "The Essayist Is Sorry for Your Loss." In *Touchstone Anthology of Contemporary Creative Nonfiction.* Edited by Lex Williford and Michael Martone. New York: Simon and Schuster, 2007.

Levis, Larry. "Winter Stars." In *Winter Stars.* Pittsburgh, Penn.: University of Pittsburgh Press, 1985.

Lindbergh, Anna. *A Year by the Sea.*

Lodato, Victor. "Jack, July." *New Yorker,* September 22, 2014.

Lopate, Phillip. "On the Necessity of Turning Oneself into a Character." In *To Show and to Tell: The Craft of Literary Nonfiction.* New York: Free Press, 2013.

———. "Portrait of My Body." *Michigan Quarterly Review,* Fall 1993.

———. "Reflection and Retrospection: A Pedagogic Mystery Story." *The Fourth Genre,* Spring 2005.

———. *To Show and to Tell: The Craft of Literary Nonfiction.* New York: Simon and Schuster, 2013.

———. "Writing Personal Essays: On the Necessity of Turning Oneself into a Character." In *Writing Creative Nonfiction: Instruction and Insights from*

Teachers of the Associated Writing Programs. Edited by Carolyn Forché and Phillip Gerard. Cincinnati, Ohio: Story Press, 2001.

———. *The Art of the Personal Essay: An Anthology from the Classical Era to the Present,* New York: Anchor Books, *1994.*

MacDonald, Helen. *H Is for Hawk.* London: Vintage, 2014.

Malcolm, Janet. "Six Glimpses of the Past: On Photography and Memory." *New Yorker,* October 22, 2018.

Manguso, Sarah. "Green-Eyed Verbs." *New York Times,* January 29, 2016.

Martin, Lee. "Kentucky." In *Turning Bones.* Lincoln: University of Nebraska Press, 2003.

McEwan, Ian. *The Child in Time.* London: Vintage, 2010.

McPhee, John. "Structure." *New Yorker,* January 14, 2013.

Mendelsohn, Daniel. *The Lost: A Search for Six of the Six Million.* New York: HarperCollins, 1983.

"Which Authors or Books Have Worked on You as 'Negative Influences?'" *New York Times Book Review,* January 21, 2014.

Michaels, Leonard. "My Yiddish." *Threepenny Review,* Fall 2003.

Miller, Brenda. "The Date." In *Seasons of the Body: Essays.* Louisville, Ky.: Sarabande Books, 2002.

———. "A Braided Heart: Shaping the Lyric Essay." In *A Braided Heart: Essays on Writing and Form.* Ann Arbor: University of Michigan Press, 2021.

Mirsky, Yehuda. *Rav Kook: Mystic in a Time of Revolution.* New Haven, Conn.: Yale University Press, 2014.

Mohn, Bent. "Talk with Isak Dinesen." *New York Times Book Review,* November 3, 1957.

Moore, Dinty. *Field Guide to Writing Flash Nonfiction.* Brookline, Mass.: Rose Metal Press, 2012.

Morgan, Robert. *Gap Creek: The Story of a Marriage.* Chapel Hill, N.C.: Algonquin Books of Chapel Hill, 1999.

Morrison, Tony. *Jazz.* London: Vintage, 2000.

Nance, Kevin. "The Deeper Mind: A Profile of Marilynne Robinson." *Poets & Writers,* November–December, 2015.

Nunez, Sigrid. *The Last of Her Kind.* London: Picador, 2006.

Oates, Joyce Carol. *The Gravedigger's Daughter.* New York: Ecco, 2008.

———. *A Widow's Story.* New York: Ecco, 2012.

Oates, Joyce Carol, and Meghan O'Rourke. "Why We Write about Grief." *New York Times,* February 26, 2011.

O'Rourke, Meghan. *The Long Goodbye: A Memoir.* New York: Riverhead Books, 2011.

———. "Story's End." *New Yorker,* March 7, 2011.

Orwell, George. *Shooting an Elephant.* London: Penguin, 2009.

Pennebaker, James. *Opening Up: the Healing Power of Expressing Emotions.* New York: Guilford, 1997.

Percy, Benjamin. "The Worst-Case Scenario." *Poet and Writers,* March–April, 2015.

Plimpton, George. "E. L. Doctorow: The Art of Fiction No. 94." *Paris Review* no. 101 (Winter 1986).

Rico, Gabriele. *Writing the Natural Way.* New York: Putnam, 2000.

Reisman, Nancy. "Moving through Time." In *Now Write! Fiction Exercises from Today's Best Writers and Teachers.* Edited by Sherry Ellis. New York: Penguin, 2006.

Sacks, Oliver. "Filter Fish." *New Yorker,* September, 2015.

Schappell, Elissa. "Review of *Safekeeping* by Abigail Thomas." *Vanity Fair,* March, 2015.

Schulman, David Y. *The Sefirot: Ten Emanations of Divine Power.* Lanham, Md.: Jason Aronson, 1996.

Shapiro, Dani. "When You Write a Memoir, Readers Think They Know You Better Than They Do." *New York Times Book Review,* June 27, 2016.

Shields, David. *Reality Hunger: A Manifesto.* New York: Random House, 2011.

Silverman, Sue William. *Fearless Confessions: A Writer's Guide to Memoir.* Athens, Ga.: University of Georgia Press, 2009.

Skloot, Rebecca. *The Immortal Life of Henrietta Lacks.* New York: Crown: 2010.

Smith, Zadie. "Joy." *New York Review of Books,* January 10, 2013.

Steinberg, Michael. "Three Things That Stopped Me in my Tracks: An Exercise in Discovery and Reflection." In *Now Write! Nonfiction.* Edited by Sherry Ellis. New York: Penguin, 2009.

Stevens, Wallace. "Notes toward a Supreme Fiction." In *The Collected Poems of Wallace Stevens.* London: Faber and Faber, 2006.

Strayed, Cheryl. *Wild: From Lost to Found on the Pacific Crest Trail.* New York: Vintage Books, 2012.

Taymor, Julie. "Spider-Man, the Lion King and Life on the Creative Edge." TED 2011, March 2011. TED video, 18:16.

Thiel, Diane. "The Minefield." In *Echolocations*. Pasadena, Calif: Story Line Press, 2000.

Thomas, Abigail. *Safekeeping: Some True Stories from a Life*. New York: Anchor Books, 2001.

———. *What Comes Next and How to Like It*. New York: Scribner, 2015.

Treisman, Deborah. "This Week in Fiction: Etgar Keret." *New Yorker,* December 15, 2011.

Vann, David. "A Conversation with Grace." *Massachusetts Review* 49, no. 4 (Winter 2008): 492–93.

White, E. B. *The Essays of E. B. White*. New York: Harper and Row, 1977.

White, Michael. *Reauthoring Lives: Interviews and Essays*. Adelaide, Australia: Dulwich Centre, 1998.

Williams, Terry Tempest. "A Letter to Deb Clow": *Red: Passion and Patience in the Desert*. New York: Pantheon, 2001. (Originally appeared in *Northern Lights* magazine as "Why I Write," Summer 1998.)

Woolf, Virginia. *The Death of the Moth*. New York: Harcourt Brace Jovanovich, 1974.

———. *A Writer's Diary: Being Extracts from the Diary of Virginia Woolfe*. Edited by Leonard Woolf. San Diego: Harvest Books, 1953.

Wright, James. "A Blessing," and "Lying in a Hammock at William Duffy's Farm in Pine Island, Minnesota." In *Above the River: The Complete Poems*. New York: Farrar, Straus and Giroux, 1990.

Young, Molly. "Letter of Appreciation: Kneipp Herbal Bath Oils." *New York Times Magazine,* April 17, 2015.

Index

ABOUT THE AUTHOR

SHERRI MANDELL is an award-winning writer who has contributed to numerous magazines and journals, including *USA Today, The Times of Israel, Hadassah Magazine,* and the *Jerusalem Post.* She is the author of several books, including a spiritual memoir, *The Blessing of a Broken Heart,* which won a National Jewish Book Award in 2004 and was translated into three languages. It was also produced as a play that toured throughout America and Israel. Her other books are *The Road to Resilience,* providing seven spiritual steps of resilience, and *Reaching for Comfort,* documenting her experience as a pastoral counselor working on the cancer ward in a hospital in Jerusalem. She is also the author of two children's picture books and teaches writing workshops online.

Mandell holds a master's degree in creative writing and studied Kabbalah with teachers in Jerusalem. For the past 20 years, she and her husband have directed the Koby Mandell Foundation in Israel whose flagship program is Camp Koby, a therapeutic sleepaway camp for bereaved children. She lives in Israel.